D1478393

DISCARDED

Cabin Pressure

Perspectives on a Multiracial America series
Series Editor: Joe R. Feagin, Texas A&M University

The racial composition of the United States is rapidly changing. Books in the series will explore various aspects of the coming multiracial society, one in which European-Americans are no longer the majority and where issues of white-on-black racism have been joined by many other challenges to white dominance.

Titles in the Series

Breaking the Code of Good Intentions, by Melanie Bush

Middle Eastern Lives in America, by Amir Mavasti and Karyn McKinney

Shades of Difference: A History of Ethnicity in America, by Richard Rees

Protecting Our Own: Race, Crime, and African Americans, by Katheryn Russell-Brown

Emotional Bridges to Puerto Rico: Migration, Return Migration, and the Struggles of Incorporation, Elizabeth M. Aranda

Structural Inequality: Black Architects in the United States, Victoria Kaplan

Globalization and America: Race, Human Rights, and Inequality, Angela J. Hattery, David G. Embrick, and Earl Smith

Adoption in a Color-Blind Society, by Pamela Anne Quiroz

Doing Business with Beauty: Black Women, Hair Salons, and the Racial Enclave Economy, by Adia Harvey Wingfield

Fade to Black and White: Interracial Images in Popular Culture, by Erica Chito Childs

Cyber Racism: White Supremacy Online and the New Attack on Civil Rights, by Jessie Daniels

Racism and Discourse in Latin America, by Teun A. van Dijk

Commodified and Criminalized: New Racism and African Americans in Contemporary Sports, by Leonard, David J. and C. Richard King

Everyday Forms of Whiteness: Understanding Race in a Post-Racial World, 2nd edition, Melanie E. L. Bush

The Urban Racial State: Managing Race Relations in American Cities, Noel A. Cazenave

Everyday Injustice: Latino Professionals and Racism, by Maria Chávez

Animating Difference: Race, Gender, and Sexuality in Contemporary Films for Children, C. Richard King, Carmen R. Lugo-Lugo, and Mary K. Bloodsworth-Lugo

The Cosby Cohort: Race, Class, and Identity among Second Generation Middle Class Blacks, Cherise A. Harris

Cabin Pressure

African American Pilots, Flight Attendants, and Emotional Labor

Louwanda Evans

ROWMAN & LITTLEFIELD PUBLISHERS, INC.
Lanham • Boulder • New York • Toronto • Plymouth, UK

Published by Rowman & Littlefield Publishers, Inc.
A wholly owned subsidiary of The Rowman & Littlefield Publishing Group, Inc.
4501 Forbes Boulevard, Suite 200, Lanham, Maryland 20706
www.rowman.com

10 Thornbury Road, Plymouth PL6 7PP, United Kingdom

British Library Cataloguing in Publication Information Available

Library of Congress Cataloging-in-Publication Data

Evans, Louwanda, 1975-
Cabin pressure : African American pilots, flight attendants, and emotional labor / Louwanda Evans.
p. cm.
Includes bibliographical references and index.
ISBN 978-1-4422-2135-2 (cloth : alk. paper) — ISBN 978-1-4422-2136-9 (ebook)
1. Airlines—United States—Employees. 2. African American professional employees. 3. Racism—United States. 4. African American air pilots. 5. Flight attendants. 6. United States—Race relations. I. Title.
HD8039.A4272U548 2013
331.6'396073--dc23 2013018699

♾™ The paper used in this publication meets the minimum requirements of American National Standard for Information Sciences Permanence of Paper for Printed Library Materials, ANSI/NISO Z39.48-1992.

Printed in the United States of America

To Norma Williams

Contents

Foreword   ix
Joe R. Feagin, Texas A & M University

Preface   xiii

Acknowledgments   xix

1   Introduction   1
2   Trapped at Thirty Thousand Feet: Infiltrating White Space   15
3   On Display at All Times: Flight Attendants   55
4   Emotional Labor and Systemic Racism   79
5   The Emotional Labor of Coping and Resistance   101
6   Conclusion   121

Notes   131

References   143

Index   147

About the Author   153

Foreword

Joe R. Feagin, Texas A & M University

Today, much of the racist world that is still the United States is intellectually covered up or sanitized by elite and ordinary white Americans. An assortment of sincere, and not so sincere, fictions parade across the vision of anyone who watches mainstream television and internet media or listens to talk radio: a post-racial America, an end of white racism, a major decline in white dominance, and significant "reverse racism." Such sanitizing notions typically appear with little or no supporting data, albeit often with a perfunctory citation of Barack Obama's election to the U.S. presidency.

One reason that such fictions about U.S. society have staying power is that white or white-vetted voices control most of the public discussion and dialogue about racial matters, as they have for centuries. What is ordinarily missing in these mainstream media analyses is the strong voice of the very Americans of color who are so frequently discussed, stereotyped, or denigrated in mainstream portrayals of U.S. racial issues.

In reading this savvy book, we encounter an innovative and critical analysis of highly original field research by a new talent in U.S. social science, the sociologist Dr. Louwanda Evans. In this analysis Evans, herself a former flight attendant, demonstrates well that there is no reality to the white fantasy of a post-racial America, that there has been no end for white racism, and that there is a high level of persisting white power and privilege. Drawing on extensive and in-depth interviewing with African American pilots and flight attendants, Evans shows that even the African American professionals that many whites and others view as proof of a post-racial America currently face substantial levels of racial discrimination and other racist mistreatment at the hands of whites of various ages, classes, and statuses.

"Success" in U.S. society, as articulated by prominent white adjudicators of the advancement of Americans of color, involves significant achievement in terms of occupation, education, and income. However, *real* success means much more than such economic and educational achievements for these black professionals. Let us consider one brief commentary from this book's many astute commentaries from black pilots and flight attendants that provide insightful glimpses into their recurring encounters with racist workplaces. In this interview quote an African American pilot with years of experience in the airline industry suggests that to succeed in terms of the norms of his corporate workplace

> you have to be a chameleon. I don't care what your personal habits are, your personal speech patterns, your behavior differences—when you walk on that property with that uniform you have to be a chameleon—you have to be almost whitewashed. That doesn't mean you change your thinking, but your behavior has to comply with that corporate culture. . . . . You have to comply or you will not survive because they can let you go for any reason whatsoever. . . . You have to just adapt to your surroundings and imitate. There are forces that do not want to see the status quo overturned. It is the mentality that you don't belong here and we're going to do what we can to make sure you don't get here. The airlines' culture was built around that.

This is one of many instructive commentaries on the realities of everyday racism that is provided by the pilots and flight attendants intensively interviewed by Evans, yet an insightful commentary that few whites in my research experience can readily understand. This veteran pilot perceptively explains or hints at several of the important themes centrally developed by Evans in this pioneering book.

For instance, here and elsewhere in these respondents' interviews, we observe the persisting and tragic reality of everyday racial discrimination, discrimination that signals black professionals do not really belong in the white-controlled work spaces of industries like this one. This discrimination is not a matter of isolated incidents with a few bigots, but of the recurring and systemic character of contemporary discrimination inside and outside the U.S. airline industry. Such persisting racism is unsurprising given the fact that, from the beginning in the early 20th century, this airline industry has been white-normed and white-controlled. This industry initially emerged after World War I during the Jim Crow era when no black pilots or entrepreneurs were allowed into positions of authority in this new industry; and nearly 100 years later African Americans, as this respondent eloquently testifies, are still often marginalized in this industry's white-normed corporate culture and structure.

Like other airline industry respondents in this book, this pilot astutely describes the reality of "success" for most people of color in these historically white institutions. There is great sadness in reports like this one, and it is a sadness for which white America bears great responsibility. The reputed progress of black professionals in society's major institutions is widely exaggerated or misunderstood by most white analysts, yet this image of progress persists with little or no critical examination as convenient image-salvaging notions for whites. Measured in strong *human rights* terms, real success in corporate workplaces like that of the airline industry should be gauged by more than a monetary standard. Real success for people of color thus should at a minimum entail meaningful acceptance without discrimination, reciprocal respect, and major cultural and structural adjustments in an industry historically normed by whites with their own group's interests in mind. As this veteran pilot suggests, real human success means, among other things, not having to deal with recurring signals that you do not belong there, that you are racially othered and inferior.

In this innovative research analysis Evans underscores the important theme of the enhanced and great emotional labor necessitated for black professionals navigating racist workplaces and associated contexts within which they live their lives. We can feel this black pilot's recurring pain in his frustrated words about imposed chameleon-like conformity and its meanings. We sense how much extra time such black professionals, in contrast to otherwise similar white professionals, must spend in emotionally and cognitively assessing the difficulties of racist workplaces and in developing the adaptive strategies necessary to survive such incessantly oppressive environments. Throughout her research, Evans shows that these experienced black airline employees do *not* lack agency in dealing with this everyday racism but, as indicated in this quote, not only spend much intellectual and emotional effort in analyzing difficult work environments but also develop some necessary coping strategies for survival. They conform strategically and reflectively when forced to do so, but they also describe, often in detail, an array of antiracist resistance strategies--some direct and planned, and others indirect or spontaneous.

Thus, one can search throughout Evans's substantial and nuanced interviews with these talented black airline professionals, but will find no evidence that we have moved into that fanciful world of "no more racism" described by white media analysts, white politicians, and others who seek to spread their self-serving fictions about this still racialized society. There are many lessons to be learned from the experiences of the courageous black female and male professionals who are well-voiced in this original and pathbreaking book, and I hope that great numbers of Americans, of many and diverse backgrounds, will find their way to it in order to understand better what a racialized America is still like for African Americans. I hope too that they reflect well upon the numerous insightful suggestions and proposals from these astute pilots and flight attendants about what should be done to end the oppressive realities of persisting white racism inside and outside U.S. workplaces.

Preface

You sure are a pretty little black girl . . . [and] it would be my pleasure to give
you the finer things in life.
—personal interaction with a first-class passenger

The opening statement captures well one of my earliest interactions with a
white male passenger on the aircraft. In the late 1990s, I started what I was
sure to be a lengthy career as a flight attendant for a major commercial
airline. Many of the thousands of interactions that I had in the course of
performing my job as a flight attendant often incorporated aspects of my
identity, as seen in the above racialized and gendered interaction. This particular type of interaction was not the first or last in which my race, gender, and
perceptions of my social class dominated the nature of my interactions with
others, specifically whites.[1]

One of my most memorable and early encounters on the aircraft, the
white male passenger mentioned above, began what he thought would be a
complimentary conversation in his stating that I was a "pretty little black
girl." As I took his coat, I replied, "So pretty comes in colors?" When I
returned for his drink order, shortly after hanging his coat, he went on to
state, "I own a brokerage firm on Wall Street." My reply was simply, "That's
great!" The final aspect of our interaction occurred when I returned to place
his beverage in between his first-class seat, and he stated, "It would be my
pleasure to give you the finer things in life." Maintaining my somewhat
stooped position, I replied in my kindest flight attendant voice, "What makes
you think I don't already have the finer things in life?" As an untrained
sociologist at the time, I was still aware that his language was problematic—I
was seen first as a "girl" and not a woman, I was compartmentalized and seen
as pretty *through* a racialized lens, and I understood well his assumption that
I would be interested in what his money could buy. There was an inherent

xiii

sense of entitlement through his attempt to touch my hand during our interaction, his mention that he is a "million miler," and in the fact that departing the aircraft he left a small box containing a gold necklace, along with his business card that stated simply: Call me. It was as though his reference to the number of miles he had flown with my airline granted him special privileges, such as access to my "little black girl" body. Immediately, I also recognized that I had no idea how to handle this sort of interaction within the context of work.[2]

Engaging in effective customer service was indeed something discussed at length during training. We discussed in detail how to handle issues with missing meals and/or beverages, how to keep passengers calm and satisfied during delays, and how to communicate with passengers about luggage, seat assignments, and disagreements with other passengers. The ability to diffuse uncomfortable situations for passengers was well articulated during training. In addition, because safety was the most important aspect of the job, we spent considerable time on first aid, aircraft and passenger safety during the course of flight, and how to effectively perform duties in the event of emergencies. The most important aspect of the job, to uphold safety standards, was often placed on the back burner during the course of the workday to attend to the passengers as we transported them to their final destinations.

Attending a lengthy training, we understood the importance of keeping passengers safe and providing great customer service. Though we were often told that our primary responsibility as flight attendants was to ensure passenger and aircraft safety, I and many other flight attendants felt that passengers had an altogether different idea of the responsibilities of flight attendants, most all of which dealt primarily with customer service issues. A result of such emphasis placed on service produced the necessity to engage in emotion work—this idea of shielding or withholding your emotions while dealing with the emotions of others. Many flight attendants became experts in hiding anger, shouting profanities without moving lips, and wearing a smile when exhausted. In other words, we were aware that there were rules in place that prevented (and prohibited) what was actually felt on the inside to be displayed on the outside. Accordingly, this not only ensured continued employment but also the contentment and hopeful return of our passengers.

While most all of the flight attendants engaged in the juggling of emotions, time on the job taught me that this side act of juggling was unequal. There was indeed an amount of superficial emotions displayed in the workplace; however, there was an aspect of the job the airline industry had not trained me for—how to handle being called racial and/or gendered derogatory epithets while at work. The airline industry had not trained me on how to deal with someone who refuses a beverage because of my race.[3] I can recall, and many of the flight attendants interviewed for this project recall well, the conversations had in the context of training about gendered interactions. It was as if gendered concerns existed in the workplace, yet race was invisible.[4] Race and ethnicity, along with several other social characteristics, were unspoken. In line with mainstream desires to render race or racialized interactions invisible, the airline industry did not mention the possibility that my race or the race of my respondents would influence how passengers would perceive our presence on the aircraft. When we received training on interacting with individuals from "diverse" backgrounds, we were never told that our "diverse" identities would be seen as problematic, not only to passengers but also by those we fly with.

One early, uncomfortable co-worker interaction came when I was having a conversation with several flight attendants as we waited on the empty aircraft between flights. At the time, I was comfortable with those flight attendants and was speaking with them about my family. Not paying much attention to my grammatical sophistication, the captain entered the aircraft, placed his bags in the flight deck, and came to the first-class cabin to make his introduction. As I am conversing with the flight attendants, he interrupts our conversation to say to me: "You need to learn to speak proper English." This racialized connection to language and dialect is something many African Americans in this project are familiar with. There are African American pilots and flight attendants who mention the narrative of black language that can render one instantaneously racialized (as in speaking improper English), or the more subtle "compliment" of "You are articulate." It is in these brief interactions that I was all too aware that what happens in real-world interactions outside of the aircraft would also contribute greatly to the performance of my job. Indeed, the workplace became an extension of my everyday life as a person of color. The key difference is that the aircraft introduced an environment in which I could not easily walk away to diffuse the situation. Once called a "black bitch" by a first-class passenger, I could go no farther than the first-class galley, and only for a few moments.

I started to think of work differently when I returned to school while still flying with the airline. One of the earliest books I read in a Formal Organizations class was *The Managed Heart: The Commercialization of Human Feeling* by Arlie R. Hochschild. The book was appealing to me specifically because it was partially about my current occupation.[5] While there was much I could agree with as it pertained to the gendered nature of flight attending, I was also aware that many of my experiences as a black woman, and the experiences of my black male flight attendant friends, was missing from the analysis. Much like the job I performed, the invisibility of race or racialized experiences assumed the normative nature of whiteness in the industry. It was from this observation in the workplace and literature that I started to think about flight attendants, and eventually, piloting, differently. I was aware that many of my white colleagues had different experiences on the aircraft. They were not concerned with being called a "black bitch," a "colored girl," or "boy," nor did they belong to the "you people" group while performing their jobs. They did not have to be concerned with how co-workers and passengers worked to exclude workers of color during the course of work. Also missing altogether in the literature was the twofold nature of work in the airline industry. The ways in which race and gender entered interactions was not limited only to interactions with passengers but were also inclusive of our interactions with one another as workers. Hochschild's notion of emotional labor—formally, that "labor used to induce or suppress personal feeling in order to sustain the outward countenance that produces the proper state of mind in others" and for the comfort of others—did not lend itself to how we engage in emotional labor when a large portion of the job extended beyond being good stewards of customer service to include much emotional labor performed as workers of color in the airline industry that result directly from our identity in the context of the industry.[6]

My position as a woman of color and past flight attendant introduced several benefits and challenges for this project. While I was granted an "insider" status in some cases, my past tenure as a flight attendant did not provide the opportunities I'd assumed it would tap into the population of flight attendants. The introduction to black flight crew members by friends still in the industry was met with the difficulties of geographical location and time off. Once several interviews were scheduled, there was an assumption that I had an in-depth familiarity with the language of the industry. During my time working for the airline industry, I had only encountered one African American male pilot, so my opportunity to gain entry into this small population was difficult. The general benefit of being a past flight attendant validated my ability to ask questions as a researcher and provided an initial, albeit surface, relationship to relative strangers. In the end, it was not my past position as a flight attendant that provided me with an insider status but my racial identity that allowed me to reach a population of black workers often unwilling to discuss race in the workplace.

As a racial insider, I found that participants in this project were open in answering questions pertaining to racism and sexism in the workplace. However, this insider status introduced new challenges to my ability to place a level of distance between my race, my participants, and my research. There were often moments where it was assumed I would understand racialized encounters. It was difficult to get participants to detail specific encounters beyond "You know what I mean" or "You know what I am talking about." While I indeed understood through my own racial ideologies, the ability to flesh out meaning in their words, not my own, was often difficult. Being granted this status, my participants would freely discuss turbulent times in the workplace as it pertained to race and gender, and many mentioned it was because they believed I could understand. But there were occasions where I asked participants to provide the details as though I inherently didn't understand that I was met with skepticism. During one interview with a pilot, he detailed that he and other black pilots were referred to as "N1, N2, and N3" at his airline. I asked that he explain in detail the meaning of N1, and he replied, "You know what N1 stands for." Asked to spell it out, he initially halted the interview and asked that I show my credentials again. He asked if I was a reporter and asked that I reiterate the purposes of my research. It was in this interaction, and several others, that my participants questioned if they had "said too much" to an insider-outsider. After all, I was no longer a flight attendant, but an outside researcher. My insider status, while providing a level of comfort to "tell all," also induced a fear that they had taken the conversation to a level that should remain buried with those in the industry of which I was no longer a member.

Navigating my identity as a researcher and as a woman of color provided great insight into the conceptual framework and structure of this book. While sharing the stories of the brave men and women that work in an industry that systemically excludes them on the basis of their intersecting racial and gender identity, we all took part in the process of engaging in emotional labor. The emotion of recalling specific events in the workplace was a painful process for my participants. There were times when those emotions reached a boiling point and I had to convince myself that those emotions, often displayed through anger and raised voices, were not aimed at me but were the result of long-standing emotional labor and devaluation in the workplace. Therefore, the primary focus of this book is to give voice to those marginalized in the industry. In this book, I seek to further develop the theory of emotional labor to be inclusive of the major role social identity plays in our interactions in the workplace. Emotional labor as currently conceptualized must be expanded to include the notion that it is *never ending* for minority populations working in occupations in which they are underrepresented. It is not an aspect of work that is secondary, but it is actually performed at all times.

Acknowledgments

As a child, my mother would often tell me: "I don't care what other people or society thinks of you—you are not destined to fail." Even as a young girl, growing up in sometimes less than ideal circumstances, I understood well the wisdom of her words. I could not have done this without a great and supportive family. Mom (Linda Mathis), Stan, Alaina (and Bob), and Phil, you are the people that truly know the huge significance of this accomplishment and how far we have come. Mom, I thank you for always encouraging me to dream, even when it was implied that "folks like us shouldn't dream." Stan, I thank you for knowing when to ask "Is everything okay?" and knowing when to step in to make sure that all is well. To my sister, Alaina, you always know what to say, even if I do not want to hear it. Our daily conversations keep me sane. To my dearest friends, Elizabeth Guillot-Jones, Akeele Johnson, and Durango Adams, you mean the world to me, and I thank you for being beacons of light when I have felt lost. Thank you for always reminding me to keep strong in my faith.

I have tremendous gratitude to my mentor and friend, Joe Feagin, for kindly taking me on as a master's student while at the University of Texas at Arlington. Joe, you have truly encouraged me in innumerable ways and have taught me that it is okay to believe in my work and myself. For this, Joe, I am most grateful. I would also like to sincerely thank Sarah Gatson and Alex McIntosh for early readings of this work. I am also indebted to Rogelio Saenz and Wendy Moore, great mentors and friends; words cannot express how thankful I am to you both. Thank you for your deep understanding and your ability to meet me on many levels. Though no longer with us, I want to thank Dr. Howard Kaplan for keeping me on my toes by encouraging me to see a multitude of perspectives in my work.

I have been encouraged and would like to thank my colleagues at Millsaps College: Professors Julian Murchison, Ming Tsui, and George Bey, I thank you all for your encouragement to finish, and I thank Julian for lending an ear when I felt overwhelmed with the data. I would also like to thank Dora Robertson for stepping in to help me out in any way possible. I would also like to thank those in the Department of Sociology at Texas A&M University, specifically Jane Sell, Christi Ramirez, Veeda Williams, Jessica Barron, and Charity Clay for their quick willingness to support me in all ways possible.

Finally, I thank and dedicate this work to Norma Williams, a fantastic scholar that departed too soon. Norma, you planted tiny seeds each time I was in your presence. I am here because you saw something others overlooked. I also send a heartfelt thanks to the numerous pilots and flight attendants participating in this project. All of you stepped in, gave me literature, and "schooled" me on the industry. You are brave men and women who I admire deeply—you are my heroes.

Chapter One

Introduction

On a flight to Reagan National Airport from Atlanta, I had an encounter with a [white] male passenger as I moved through the aisle with the beverage cart. I reached his row, stopped the cart, and asked, "Can I get you something to drink?" "Would you mind getting someone else to bring me my drink? I would prefer you not touch my cup." Initially, I thought that maybe it was something religious and based on my gender because we get that sometimes. But then a white female flight attendant served him his Coke with no problems. I was shocked and upset, and as a matter of fact, I did not want him to have a drink at all!
—Sue, senior black flight attendant

My trip had ended, and I was trying to catch a ride home on another airline . . . I was sitting at the gate in my pilot's uniform, just sitting there, and an older white man got up and went to the gate and said, "That nigger better not be flying my plane."[1]
—Tim, pilot

Sue met the male stranger near the end of her two-day trip. As Sue recalls this example, she is sure to mention the unfortunate commonality of being denied the ability to perform a major aspect of her job as a flight attendant— that of providing customer service. Sue, like the many other African American flight attendants interviewed in this project, consider the denial of their service to be connected to their racial identity as well as their gender identity.[2] Tim, in an altogether different position on the aircraft, carries the burden to prove his skills and worth as a pilot much like he carries his flight manual; it follows him everywhere once he enters his workplace, even when he is not actually working. The above encounters exemplify the thoughts and experiences of many African Americans currently employed in the commercial aviation industry. Working in completely different facets of the industry

1

and requiring different skills, both positions of flight attendant and pilot carry a tacit obligation to perform some form of emotional labor.[3] This unpaid aspect of work remains largely invisible until performed unsatisfactorily.[4] Moreover, the ability of these African Americans in the airline industry to perform their jobs and the perception that they are performed efficiently hinges on much more than their ability to make safe landings and serve beverages, but they often incorporate aspects of their identity in the evaluation of performance.

Situated within the context of the airline industry, and recalling the opening quote made by Tim, emotional labor for many African Americans in the airline industry does not only occur within the microcosm of work—it is also performed *outside* of work and is directly connected to the racialized narratives of race and gender, preexisting ideologies of what represents a *pilot*, and the institutional culture of the industry. Imagine for a moment the perspective and experience of Tim—the private and visible experience of being called a "nigger" in a public space, while in uniform and held to the restrictions of the organization even though he is no longer performing any work duties. The use of this particular racial epithet invokes the brutal reality of racism and challenges Tim's right and ability to wear the uniform and fly the airplane while removing from Tim the ability to react emotionally or verbally to this unnerving statement. Noteworthy here is that there were no consequences for the white male passenger; he was not asked to leave the area or denied service. He received no open response from Tim or his co-workers or from others at the gate. Thus, the restrictive requirement of being emotionally controlled while in uniform systematically places Tim in the unfortunate position of engaging in and reproducing a discourse of racial oppression.[5] Collectively, this emotional labor as a part of work is deeply intertwined with social identity and is a manifestation of larger structural beliefs about race and gender. The use of the "n" word, and the comfort in which the white male uses it openly, places the ghosts of our past in a contemporary reality.

EMOTIONAL LABOR AND FEELING RULES

Emotional labor as a theoretical framework was examined in the 1983 work *The Managed Heart: Commercialization of Human Feeling* by Arlie R. Hochschild. Hochschild conceptualized emotional labor to be the management of "feeling to create a publicly observable facial and bodily display; emotional labor is sold for a wage and therefore has exchange value" (Hochschild 1983:7). Hochschild continues her conceptualization of emotional labor and notes that

> this labor requires one to induce or suppress feeling in order to sustain the outward countenance that produces the proper state of mind in others . . .

This kind of labor calls for a coordination of mind and feeling, and it sometimes draws on a source of self that we honor as deep and integral to our individuality.

One goal of Hochschild's research was to view occupations "from the point of view of understanding the relation of gender to jobs, and to understand the problems of women as workers and how they are confounded with the problems of being a minority in a given occupation" (Hochschild 1983:15). Emotional labor is much like physical labor—it is sold for a wage in many industries where there is ongoing interaction or "service work." It is an altogether public act—moving from emotion management that occurs privately to something inherently public when it is required and "controlled" by employers as a formal job requirement (Hochschild 1983).[6]

Emotion, as seen by Hochschild (1979:551), is the "bodily cooperation with an image, a thought, a memory—a cooperation of which the individual is aware," and feelings, as a component of emotions, are "not stored 'inside' us, and they are not independent of acts of management."[7] The management of emotions contributes to the creation of emotion and thereby becomes a method of communicating information. Guided by "feeling rules," these rules vacillate between *what I should feel* and *what I do feel*, establishing the sense of entitlement or obligation that governs emotional exchanges. Situated within the social structure, these rules are indeed culturally determined by the situation, thereby describing normative expression of the appropriate type and amount of feeling to be displayed in any given situation or environment.[8] Succinctly, Hochschild posits,

> A feeling rule shares some formal properties with other sorts of rules, such as rules of etiquette, rules of bodily comportment, and those of social interaction in general. A feeling rule is like these other kinds of rules in the following ways: It delineates a zone within which one has permission to be free of worry, guilt, or shame with regard to the situated feeling . . . Feeling rules differ curiously from other types of rules in that they do not apply to action but to what is often taken as a precursor to action . . . Feeling rules reflect patterns of social membership. (Hochschild 1979:564–65)[9]

Much like those normative rules that govern behavior, feeling rules are subject to sanctioning and are thus another system of social control within the workplace. Differing by social membership, and feelings, even without action, are culturally and socially scripted, and they are broken down by gender, racial-ethnic identity, social class, and other social characteristics. By combining these feeling rules and organizational norms of feeling with intersecting identities, these rules become less clear but nevertheless serve as the foundation on which emotions, specifically emotional display and emotional labor, are based. Collectively, even though feeling rules and emotion norms are socially and structurally situated, it is noteworthy that not all social groups are responsible for the creation or enforcement of these rules of feeling and emotion.

Since the publication of Hochschild's pivotal work, much has been done on gender, gendered occupations, and emotional labor.[10] However, only recently have studies begun to incorporate racial-ethnic identity in a way to suggest different types of emotional labor. In her evaluation on the sociology of emotional labor, Amy Wharton (2009:152) notes,

> The deference expected of workers in front-line service jobs raises important issues of race and class, as well as gender . . . Deference—or the capacity to place oneself in a "one down" position vis-à-vis others—is a characteristic demanded of all those in disadvantaged structural positions, including women, racial-ethnic minorities, and others in subordinate statuses. When deference is made a job requirement, members of structurally disadvantaged groups are likely to be overrepresented in such jobs or even be seen as better suited for the work than members of more advantaged groups.

For example, Millian Kang's work (2003, 2010) on the emotional and body labor performed by Korean immigrant nail salon workers formulates the connections and intersections between gender, race, and class that workers encounter while working with diverse populations. Noting that many consumers often refer to owners as "Asian or Oriental" without referencing an ethnic identity elicits the age-old stereotypical notions of Asian women as docile and productive workers, "making them desirable and exploitable in an increasingly feminized, impoverished, and unprotected labor force" (2003:824). Kang augments the literature on gendered and ethnic emotional labor and incorporates the crosscutting relationships with consumers of multiple racial and class backgrounds. With this, the expectations of service and emotion work are as much a product of the larger relationships between structural power and racial identity. Indeed, the race or ethnicity of the worker providing the service is inherently connected with the race (as well as the gender and social class) of the consumer purchasing the service and can serve as a guideline of expectations on behalf of both parties.

Intersecting identities of gender and race often create the "emotional proletariat," or those "service workers who perform face-to-face or voice-to-voice service work, while having no control over the 'feeling rules' that guide their emotional labor."[11] In addition, the emotional proletariat are those who "are in a subservient position vis-à-vis the customers"[12] and are often faced with how their social identities (in terms of race/ethnicity and gender) influence the likelihood that management will perceive that members with specific social identities are capable or incapable of actually performing specific jobs. Along these lines, consumers often "translate race and ethnic markers into indicators of the nature of the service itself."[13] Though these particular works focus mainly on "gendered" and "raced" low-wage occupations, we can presume that racial and ethnic "markers" can be carried into most occupational environments, thereby influencing both customer expectations and interactions. Consequently, "gender and ethnic identity become salient not in *whether* the worker can produce the expected emotional display, but in *how much* emotional labor this requires, and in how congruent or incongruent this display is with their sense of identity and dignity."[14]

Building on the literature in this area, Adia Wingfield (2010) examines emotional displays by African Americans in professional settings and determines that some emotional displays, when committed by African Americans, are deemed inappropriate, even though whites sometimes display these emotions as well. Take the following example provided in Wingfield's (2010:259) study of black professionals:

> Respondents suggest that a different set of feeling rules apply to them altogether wherein they are not permitted to show anger under any circumstances. They cite numerous examples of white workers who have openly expressed feelings of frustration or annoyance in ways that they believe are simply unavailable to them as black employees. Respondents argue that as black professionals, they would be punished for displaying anger in the same ways their white colleagues do.

In this example, black professionals are often held to a different set of feeling rules, a script that subjugates organizational norms of feeling and emotional labor with general social scripts of feeling and emotion that are found in the larger discursive narrative about feeling and identity. Consequently, even when feelings are normative, they are more normative within specific identity characteristics and are not equally applied, suggesting that workers of color must simultaneously engage organizational rules of feeling and emotional labor as well as those group-specific rules of feeling and labor. These workers therefore face the complex challenge of upholding normative organizational rules that are unequally applied, giving supremacy to the feelings of others, while reproducing the explicit inequality of feeling and emotional labor in the workplace. The outcome is that they are forced to sacrifice the ability to construct new feeling rules in organizations that fail to incorporate and acknowledge the validity of their feelings, and emotional labor.

African Americans carry the awareness of the often negative stereotypes surrounding them and their emotions. Therefore, they are likely to rely on various mechanisms to ensure they do not display emotions, although the emotions are often appropriate, in specific environments. In her work on elite law schools, Wendy Moore (2008) details the costs associated for students of color at elite, predominantly white, law schools. Dealing largely with the experiences of students of color and the existing relationships between faculty and other students, Moore (2008) notes that students of color in these environments must constantly engage in an ongoing daily struggle against institutional spaces with deeply racialized (white) norms. The high cost of this emotional labor is one that students of color are required to pay in the pursuit of their education—one that is not equally shared with their white counterparts. In a similar vein, many of the students understand that if they provide a retort based on emotion, they are seen negatively, with an image that coincides with already negative perceptions of African Americans in general. Consequently, African Americans remain either estranged or in a perpetual state of emotional turmoil.[15]

THE NATURE OF EXCLUSIONARY INSTITUTIONS: AN INTRODUCTION TO SYSTEMIC RACISM

It is significant that the black pilot in the opening was called a blatant racist epithet in a major airport, and it is also significant that consumers can openly refuse a beverage from a black flight attendant. As many major airlines as well as other major industries now tout great advances in the diversity of their workforce, the mainstream American public is also more likely to accept the dominant narrative of race neutrality and equal opportunity.[16] These collective narratives simultaneously marginalize the discriminatory experiences of people of color and women and uphold white male racial and emotional supremacy. However, racial-ethnic minorities and women, in any significant numbers, continue to face barriers to more prestigious positions on our nation's top aircraft. Indeed, the position of pilot remains overwhelmingly associated with masculinity and whiteness, and that of flight attendant is associated with a racialized femininity.[17] During the 1950s and 1960s, the airline industry came under attack for its lack of African American flight attendants and pilots. Subsequently, Ruth Carol Taylor, an African American woman, was hired in 1958 as a flight attendant, and following a landmark 1963 Supreme Court case, Marlon Green became the first African American pilot to be hired by a major airline.[18] Due to institutional discrimination, the commercial airline industry, specifically in terms of pilots, remains overwhelmingly white. Currently, the airline industry employs approximately seventy-one thousand pilots with the total estimated number of African American pilots remaining under seven hundred—less than twenty of which are African American females.[19] In 2010, African American flight attendants accounted for about 14 percent of the flight attendant population, with whites at 70 percent[20] (American Community Survey 2011). In the 1980s, male flight attendants were only about 15 percent of the flight attendant population, but in 2007, they accounted for approximately twenty-six per one hundred female flight attendants (Saenz and Evans 2009).[21]

To effectively examine these historically white workspaces, the role of race and gender identity, and the consequent emotional labor, it is important to also understand how and why these institutions adhere to cultural practices that overwhelmingly value and perpetuate the taken-for-granted racial identity of whiteness. Even as the mainstream public and those inherently in power within workplaces replace most blatant discriminatory practices with narratives of color blindness, whites in many major industries can continue to express negative sentiments and hostility toward people of color, while simultaneously referencing increased diversity in the workplace to show that inequality is not about race. This produces what Eduardo Bonilla-Silva calls "racism without racists."[22] The changing nature of race narratives, found in the increasing popularity of "postracial" sociopolitical conversations, seeks to render invisible the reality that racism is institutional, political, and social—collectively, racism is *systemic*. In the airline industry and arguably many others, white normativity has developed and is maintained through the direct connections with institutional discrimination and racism. In addition, because the nature of this industry is one that was built on racist and sexist foundations of exclusion, these practices and norms are an overall part of the system, contributing to the dual and pervasive nature of racial and gendered discrimination and the unequal distribution of emotional labor performed by people of color.[23]

Systemic racism provides a necessary framework in which to understand many interactions that occur between crew members of color and passengers or co-workers. By thinking of the aircraft as a "mini society" in the air, we can learn much about these interactions by delving into the intricacies of racialized and gendered norms grounded in U.S. social structure. In the case of the United States, racial oppression has been demonstrated to be both foundational and systemic, and the oppression of people of color has been one part of our deep social structure.[24] For many middle-class African Americans, such as those pilots and flight attendants in this study, "white racism is not an abstraction generated by a militant ideology but rather a matter of ordinary experience."[25] Accordingly, it is important to examine here the nature of racism in the United States in order to understand how and why experiences such as those mentioned in this chapter opening remain recorded.

To understand systemic racism, Joe Feagin (2006) posits that the nature of racial relations go far beyond individual bigotry. Racism, along with oppression, is systemic; that is, it is a "social, material, and ideological reality that is well-embedded in major U.S. institutions," as well as in the minds of our many citizens (2006:2). Moreover, by taking a historical glimpse at the conditions in which our country was founded—one where people of color and women were relegated to subordinate positions—the contemporary picture of gender and racial inequality becomes clearer. With women and people of color assigned to inferior and subordinate positions, deeply framed stereotypical notions of their character, propensities, and abilities were also created as a means to justify oppression. Within U.S. culture, "racist and sexist ideologies permeate the social structure to such a degree that they become hegemonic, namely, seen as natural, normal, and inevitable."[26] By systematically excluding white women and people of color, the foundation of sexism and racism was deeply embedded into this country at the very onset of the development of most all of the major institutions.

Over time, the ideologies of the inferior nature of women and people of color remained reinforced through various outlets. From the founding of our country, the belief in the inferiority of black intelligence, work ethic, and general character was devised as a method of control and as a rationalization for oppression. Intrinsic in language, a color-coded ideology and discourse materialized early on through everyday interactions and had a "trickling" effect on larger society. As Feagin notes:

> Consciously or unconsciously, a majority of whites have long extended language and understandings to discuss, defend, or prescribe the hierarchy in which whites are generally dominant and people of color are generally subordinated. They have accented and honed the common folk model of a "natural" social order, what has historically been called the "great chain of being." This perspective views men as superior to women, Westerners to non-Westerners, and whites to people of color. (2006:29–30)

As this project is about emotions and the emotional labor of African American flight crews, the importance of understanding the intrusive nature of racial and gendered ideologies on interactions will remain a primary focus in social research. An aspect of systemic racism and the underlying necessity of comprehending racial and gendered ideologies must be extended to what Feagin (2010) terms the *white racial frame*. The white racial frame is indeed useful in this analysis as it can serve as the "glue" that melds together our historical and contemporary racial realities. As our interactions are indeed guided by our ideologies, I believe it fitting here to provide a brief analysis of the white racial frame. Much of this will be discussed and expanded in later chapters.

THE WHITE RACIAL FRAME

The white racial frame is an old, white-created frame that provides an overarching and destructive view on racial matters. Feagin (2010) notes that in this broad racial frame, white Americans have historically combined at least these important features: "racial stereotypes (a belief aspect), racial narratives and interpretations (integrating cognitive aspects), racial images (a visual aspect) and language accents (an auditory aspect), racialized emotions (a feelings aspect), and inclinations to discriminatory action" (2010:10–11). Over centuries of operation, this strong racial framing has encompassed both a strong positive orientation to whites and whiteness and a negative orientation to those racial "others" who are exploited and oppressed. Today, as many whites move through their everyday lives, they often combine these features in their actions and decisions in regard to Americans of color.

The white racial frame has been in existence for the bulk of our history and was often used as a method of highlighting white virtue and morality. This frame was the primary mechanism used in the exploitation of people of color and served as a catalyst for the rationalization and continued exploitation and oppression that is all too familiar in our history. For the frame to exist and survive, prepackaged notions of race are passed on not only through familial networks but also are encompassed in every major institution from politics to religion. From the first century of European colonization, "the class and patriarchal (gender) frames of oppression have been linked to the white racial frame or even nested within it" (Feagin 2010:15).

By receiving such strong support in our major institutions, the white racial frame has remained, albeit reworked in some ways. Aspects of the white racial frame have indeed been reworked and reworded but have consistently remained a dominant frame of reference for many whites. Feagin (2010) notes that the white racial frame "is an 'ideal-type,' a composite whole with a large array of elements that in everyday practice are drawn on *selectively* by white individuals acting to impose or maintain racial identity, privilege, and dominance vis-à-vis people of color in everyday interactions" (14). In this, the centuries-old negative perceptions of people of color and the positive perceptions of whites is recalled, relied upon, and often influences face-to-face interactions. Moreover, the white racial frame does not exist apart from our everyday experiences—in truth, it is essentially a part of our larger system of racial oppression.

THE INTERSECTION OF
SYSTEMIC RACISM AND EMOTIONAL LABOR

To introduce the idea and extreme importance of weaving in systemic racism and racial framing with emotional labor, I think it is fitting here to detail an account provided by a flight attendant in Hochschild's book, *The Managed Heart*:

> There was one time when I finally decided that somebody had it coming. It was a woman who complained about absolutely everything. I told her in my prettiest voice, "We're doing our best for you. I'm sorry you aren't happy with the flight time. I'm sorry you aren't happy with our service." She went on and

on about how terrible the food was, how bad the flight attendants were, how bad her seat was. Then she began yelling at me and my coworker friend, who happened to be black. "You nigger bitch!" she said. Well that did it. I told my friend not to waste her pain. (1983:114)

In this account, it is essential to briefly examine the black woman that this passenger was referencing (who, by the way, was not afforded the opportunity to tell her own story). Though this scenario was told from an observer (a white female flight attendant), it is important to note the language, connotations, and the emotional consequence of this interaction. To be yelled at in such a negative and derogatory manner, in front of co-workers and passengers alike, suggests a deeper connection between gender, race, and the emotional labor performed by African American workers in their everyday interactions. For this African American woman, as well as many others, the fact that "two innate and inerasable traits, being both black and female" are elicited reminds us of existing statuses in society.[27] Also of significant importance here is the perspective of the white flight attendant recounting the story. As she tells her black female co-worker not to "waste her pain," it is clear that she does not *understand or share* the pain of being a "nigger bitch" in public. The often intersecting nature of race and gender and the specific racial epithet used are but deeper connections to specific forms of racial and gender oppression.

TOWARD A DEEPER UNDERSTANDING OF EMOTIONAL LABOR

Thus, in this work I intend to build on the theory of emotional labor by accounting for the multifaceted way in which it is performed. Here, I suggest emotional labor is not performed in a vacuum but is instead a process that should account for the *context* in which it is performed, those interactions in which emotional labor must occur, and the simultaneous narratives that guide our interactions. Arguably, most other works on emotional labor often fail to incorporate the multiple ways it is performed throughout the workday. By specifically examining African American pilots and flight attendants, occupations that remain understudied, the more explicit connections between emotional labor performance, and race and gender identity and ideologies clearly show that much emotional labor takes place within complex systems of interaction. It is a process that is engaged in interactions with consumers and co-workers as well as with management. This focus differs from the work done by and on others as it features people of color and contextualizes their experiences in organizational environments in which they are in positions that are not seen as "typical" and are thus viewed as "less suited" for the job. Therefore, emotional labor in the traditional sense is replaced as the normative rules within the organizational culture, for people of color are not always connected directly to organizational norms of emotional display but are pulled from societal "rules" based on gendered and racialized emotion norms. Consequently, when African Americans do not adhere to normative rules for emotional display and feeling rules within the organization, they are inexplicably seen as "deviant," which carries an altogether different set of consequences. Based on stereotypes of both black male and female emotional displays, images of the "violent black male" or the "bitchy black female" permeate interactions in the workplace not only with consumers but also with co-workers and management.

Emotional labor is therefore multidimensional in that labor by people of color, in this historically white industry, is both gendered and raced; it is performed within the context of work as well as within the context of relationship management, all within an inescapable environment. For African Americans in this industry, emotional labor is connected to much more than service work; it is connected to the uniform and the aircraft as well as to the racial and gender identity of the worker and consumer. To fully comprehend the invisible and unpaid labor in dealing with the public, I argue that emotional labor and the process through which it operates cannot be separated from the larger structural conditions and ideologies in which it is required. Indeed, to understand the experiences of African Americans and emotional labor in the airline industry, it is important to deconstruct the industry and its foundation and normative organizational structures, as well as those feeling rules that exist in the industry. Here, these micro interactions that occur between black crew members and those interactions they engage in are reflective of the structural conditions of American society in general, found through the preexisting narratives of what constitutes flight attendants and pilots, women and men, and whites and racial-ethnic groups.

Herein, this work becomes necessary for understanding the experiences of people of color in the workplace. According to recent publications on women and minorities in upper management, change, though consistently slow, has happened in many industries.[28] Still underrepresented in many major industries, as people of color and women move into specific industries, their experiences of engaging in emotional labor, arguably based on their racial and gender identity, should be a primary focus of gauging the overall change, or lack thereof, of the general racial and sexist climate.

The amount of time spent in the workplace is also significant here. As the workplace is important in establishing economic stability, not much has been done to examine the personal costs to persons of color engaging in emotional labor. Ultimately, I focus primarily on the emotional labor performed within interactions with consumers, co-workers, and management that are based on identity.[29] The intersecting identities of race, gender, and class influence experiences with emotional labor and emotion work, and they are deeply connected to what we are *allowed* to feel and display. Feeling rules, though culturally determined, were not collectively created but were created and enforced by those with social power, specifically within this organization. Important here is the exclusionary foundation in which many major industries in the United States were created, suggesting that people of color had no significant input in their creation but are yet expected to uphold these feeling rules. Feeling rules and other normative cultural structures developed in this institution have persisted through a collective social reproduction of racial power, privilege, and racialized emotion norms. Much is done through contemporary racial framing of racialized and gendered "others," while there are also institutional pressures that actively reproduce inequality by forcing conformity at institutional and individual levels. For African Americans in institutionally white spaces, the discursive reproduction of white male and/or female privilege is as much an aspect of performing emotional labor on the job as those preexisting expectations of emotion work found in job descriptions. Moreover, as a result of these emotion norms and feeling rules, what is seen as private emotion work transforms to a deeper level of cognitive labor, that labor necessary to deconstruct racist and sexist views imposed by others in interactions, much before it produces emotional labor.[30]

Understanding contemporary emotion norms and displays vis-à-vis their creation allows for a deeper understanding of their perpetuation within organizations and the consequence to minority group members, women, and their successful emotional labor. As more workers integrate the workplace, recent research suggests that racial attitudes, specifically against African Americans, have not changed much in recent years and that a majority of Americans now hold explicit antiblack attitudes.[31] Consequently, it is important to build on and move emotional labor as a conceptual understanding of performing service work to one that also examines the emotional labor required in the workplace to *resist* sexism and racism or other forms of institutional discrimination. Therefore, emotional labor as a new form of social control and forced conformity on people of color in predominantly white institutions is a *double shift*, one that is performed simultaneously by women and people of color in excess to preexisting job duties.

Of significant importance herein is my goal to develop and add to the existing works on emotional labor by focusing on the often racialized and gendered experiences of these flight crews, specifically racialized emotional labor. African Americans entering our nation's aircraft in recent years introduce new bodies into a well-established, historically white organizational regime. Therefore, only examining emotional labor—that resulting from providing a service—altogether misses the bulk and severity of emotional labor performed as a direct result of entry into an organizational culture and structure in which both racial and gender identity are non-normative and seen as threatening. Placing emotional labor in this context and examining experiences with racism and sexism will serve as a contextual lens through which to view the emotional perspectives and labor performed by these individuals. The nature and setup of the aircraft itself serves as a rich location for understanding social interactions. As one respondent mentioned, "The airplane is like a mini-society inside. You have different representations of people and all their attitudes in a *confined* space." Surely, this space is more confined when looking into the cockpit, specifically when factoring in many of the changes that have taken place since September 11, 2001.[32] Thus, pilots are not only confined to a small space but also one in which there is no clear or easy escape.

I argue that in order to fully understand emotional labor as performed in the airline industry, that labor must be first understood in the context in which it is developed. There should be recognition of the big picture—"the reality of this whole society being founded on, and firmly grounded in, oppression targeting people of color now for several centuries. Given that deep underlying reality of this society, all racial-ethnic relationships and events, past and present, must be placed within that racial oppression context in order to be fully understood."[33]

What this research adds is a broader understanding of the emotional labor performed by African American women and men in roles where they are observably and numerically underrepresented. Because of this underrepresentation, there is a visceral reaction by passengers of simultaneous hypervisibility and invisibility.[34] Hypervisibility is to be observed (and pointed out) as an anomaly, consistent with being on display. Invisibility works in an opposite way—to be invisible is to experience the visceral reaction of being rendered to a position of subordinate status. It is created to reiterate the ill acknowledgment of presence while reifying the normative nature of whiteness in the industry. Noted by many, this idea of black visibility extends beyond those working on the aircraft and also includes the component of the traveling public itself. Interactions in the terminal and on the aircraft are unique for these flight crews—they are constantly "noticed" and commented on, making them hypervisible, but they simultaneously somehow become invisible to those around them. To lay out a more encompassing theory of emotional labor, I include the personal narratives of three dozen African American pilots and flight attendants currently employed with major commercial airlines.[35] I start these next few chapters with the racialized and gendered experiences of African American men and women in the workplace, followed by a more encompassing theory of emotional labor—one that shows that emotional labor is not void of organizational normative structures, specifically as evaluations of performance and interactions are based on social identity. In chapter 2, I examine and detail the current experiences of the African American pilots. This chapter takes an in-depth look at the consequences of the preexisting racial and gender ideologies that creep into interactions in the workplace. The experiences of African American men and women as they enter a very white male space carries a discourse in which they must constantly engage. This chapter is followed by the more public experiences of flight attendants in chapter 3. The final chapters reformulate existing research on emotional labor by incorporating the multiple dimensions necessary when factoring in the collectivity of race and gender. Examining the emotional labor performed based on the harsh reality of racial-ethnic and gender discrimination in the workplace adds multiple new levels of emotional labor—that labor that is performed to resist discriminatory practices and maintain the stability and sanity of the self, all of which usually occur without any strong or significant institutional support.

Chapter Two

Trapped at Thirty Thousand Feet: Infiltrating White Space

The airline industry, like most major industries in the United States, has yet to incorporate diversity in any significant form. Examining the big picture of the airline industry finds that African Americans, specifically those working as pilots, still find themselves only partially represented, with their total remaining under seven hundred out of seventy-one thousand. The overall prevalence of white males in the airline industry is one result of systemic racism and discrimination in hiring and a culture that indeed gave heavy emphasis to the white and male nature of flying.[1] To date, not much research has been conducted on the experiences of African American pilots or the emotional labor performed within the context of their work. Important here is the notion that emotional labor extends beyond the performance of work only in relation to consumers, but shows the complexities of interacting directly or indirectly with consumers, co-workers, and management.

Gaining professional entry onto the aircraft and into the flight deck is indeed a rather recent achievement, though African Americans were among the numerous pioneers of flight (Hansen and Oster 1997). In this, African Americans are a unique group to study in reference to the airline industry, as many of the long-standing politics of exclusion remain strictly in place. For instance, a publication in 1995 by *Time* magazine noted that the airline industry is one that is dominated by white males, as they made up approximately 97 percent of all airline pilots. Published some ten years later, an article published by Karen Ashcraft finds that between 95 and 98 percent of commercial aviation pilots are men and 98 percent are white, and as recently as 2010, African American pilots were still less than 1 percent of commercial aviation pilots.[2] Of extreme importance here is the underrepresentation of women and racial-ethnic minorities as well as the systemic nature in which

15

white males dominate this facet of the airline industry. As much of the research on emotional labor involves industries that are gendered and/or racialized, African American pilots are entering an industry that is both gendered, in terms of masculinity, and racialized, in terms of whiteness. The experiences of African American pilots illustrate the interlocking nature of oppression because the industry was designed for and by white males. African American pilots pose an altogether unique situation; they do not "fit" the description of what has historically or contemporarily been representative of "pilot." Those black women and men working in this industry also have to contend with the long-standing ideology surrounding the occupation of pilot—one largely held by the mainstream white public to be an occupation largely performed and better performed by white males—while also dealing with racialized understandings of what is thought to be representative of appropriate "black" work and/or positions. Outside of racial identity, women in this industry have faced large-scale discrimination based on systemic sexism and the ideology that aviation, in terms of flying, was not an appropriate sphere for them.[3] As a result of court cases in the 1960s, American Airlines became the first major airline to voluntary hire a black male pilot in 1964. There were no women hired commercially until 1973, and the first African American woman was hired in 1978, some fifteen years after the pivotal 1963 Supreme Court case in which Marlon Green challenged the hiring practices of commercial airlines.[4]

FOR WHITES ONLY: AFRICAN AMERICAN PILOTS AND METHODS OF EXCLUSION

The ability to perform emotional labor based on racial and gender identity in the airline industry is something African American pilots learn early in the process of entering the industry. The painful reality of dealing with racism and sexism on a consistent basis results in an accumulation of emotional experiences—those tacked on to the emotion work required of airline employees. The racial and gendered microaggressions occurring within a typical day of work for these pilots is indeed indicative of the painful reality of working in an industry in which they have been systemically excluded. Often, the reiteration of the flight deck as reserved for white males starts at training and continues throughout the career of these crew members.

When discussing what it means to be a pilot, one African American immediately states:

> The difference between being a black pilot and being a white pilot is that if you're a white pilot the assumption is that you know what you're doing. If you're a black pilot, the assumption is [that] you don't know what you're

doing. The white pilot is to make a jackass out of himself; the black pilot is to prove he's not a jackass. You are assumed to be inept.

As I mentioned earlier, for many decades, the commercial aviation industry was one that excluded African Americans as both pilots and flight attendants. This exclusion resulted from systemic racism coupled with white framing that deemed African Americans intellectually inferior. African Americans have only begun to make any noticeable strides in entering the industry, and even so, this progress has been slow. Though African Americans are represented currently, albeit in small numbers, the commercial aviation industry remains one that is spatially segregated by type of occupation, with those working on the aircraft being reminded that the airplane is indeed a white space and reserved largely for whites. In her conceptualization of white space, Wendy Moore (2008:28) notes,

> Set in motion by the history of exclusion but remaining relevant today, racially disparate demographics of a space become a relevant (though neither necessary nor sufficient) aspect of white institutional space. Just as the racial makeup of segregated neighborhoods signifies racial space, so, too, in institutions . . . , the vast underrepresentation of people of color becomes a signifier. . . . Because most people in these institutions fail to make the connection between historical racist exclusion and contemporary institutional norms, much of the white frame remains tacit, thereby reifying whiteness within the space without need for intentional action to do so.

The spatial reality of racism and the idea that specific spaces remain designated for whites is crucial in my analysis largely because this is indicative of the experiences many African Americans face even before becoming commercial aviation pilots. In their research on the aviation industry, Janet Hansen and Clinton Oster (1997:117) note,

> The most far-reaching, longest running, and highest profile court case ended only in 1995; it involved United, which was sued, along with five of the unions with which it bargained collectively, by the U.S. attorney general in 1973. . . . The lawsuit charged United and its unions with "a pattern and practice of discrimination in hiring, termination, and other job related practices, based upon race, national origin and sex in violation of Title VII of the Civil Rights Act of 1964."

The significance of this and other court cases shed light on the discriminatory and often prejudicial experiences African Americans face in this industry. Many of the exclusionary practices of the airlines are often perpetuated at various levels, not merely only from management. Many white actors, those serving as instructors in flight schools as well as those that are currently flying in the flight deck, serve as active carriers of the message and ideology of the flight deck as one reserved for whites. Often this is done in both subtle and overt ways. These interactions serve as constant reminders to these African Americans that their work environment can be seen as an unsafe space, one where these workers do not feel free to be emotionally expressive. Here, it is important to highlight how the aircraft itself plays a role in the emotional labor performed by African Americans in this white space. Consider that once the aircraft has left the ground, pilots are indeed confined, with limited options to remove themselves from difficult and strenuous encounters. The confined aspect of the environment is even more pronounced for pilots, as leaving the flight deck is not always a viable option. A more accurate and vivid way to understand the confined nature of the aircraft is that once you take off, there is no getting off until you land! Time spent in this confined environment can indeed range up to several hours when flying internationally.

As understood by those working on the aircraft, the captain has the ultimate authority to make decisions. Even more widely acknowledged by those in the industry, the rank of captain carries a tacit and explicit level of power, prestige, and authority. In the flight deck, the pilot is followed by the first officer (FO) and/or flight engineer. Though operating differently, flight attendants also have a positional hierarchy on the aircraft (discussed in chapter 3), but contextually, flight attendants are also bound under the authority of the captain, as are all others on board, including passengers.[5] In this chapter, I focus on interactions pilots have involving both passengers and co-workers. Following closely the research of Hochschild (1983), I add the perspective of co-worker interactions as another dimension of performing emotional labor, as this is a large part of functioning as a pilot or flight attendant—one that is often missed. The relationships of male pilot/female flight attendant mirrors other co-worker emotional labor situations, such as boss/secretary, where the secretary is often described as the "office wife."[6]

RACE AS A DIMENSION OF EMOTIONAL LABOR

Much of the literature on emotional labor examines the experiences of women in the workforce, specifically in those industries providing some sort of services. As stated in the previous chapter, the work of Kang (2010) found that consumers develop an overarching expectation of who occupies certain industries based on racial and gendered stereotypes. Similarly, with African Americans working in the airline industry, the vast majority continue to find themselves employed in low-wage, unskilled positions.[7] Indeed, this remains the larger expectation of African Americans specifically when examining the industry (and other industries as well)—to be working in those unskilled positions and not in the flight deck. This ideology, based largely on our history of systemic racism, is pervasive and indeed resides in the minds of passengers as well as airline workers. And much of what African American airline workers experience emotionally and the emotional labor that they perform often hinge on social identities, particularly those salient factors of race and gender. These factors carry both internal and external meanings for individuals and groups, and the consequences of deploying and experiencing these hierarchically grounded social identities are real and have an emotional, physical, and mental cost.

This chapter introduces the idea of the interconnectivity of emotional labor and systemic racism and sexism. Many aspects of emotional labor cannot be understood apart from the experiences that call for emotion management. In this regard, though a relatively small proportion of respondents discussed flight emergencies as an aspect of the job that calls for emotional labor, the overwhelming majority openly discussed racialized and/or gendered experiences as a frequent occurrence that called for emotional labor and emotional suppression. For these African American pilots, emotions that arise in the workplace cannot be understood fully outside of the mechanisms that produce them; in performing emotional labor, aspects of identity such as race and gender often facilitate and dictate how emotional labor is performed and expressed. As I mentioned above, African American flight crew members' experiences dealing with racial and gendered identity extend well beyond the scope of being on the aircraft itself, and they incorporate these experiences into their workplace identities even before they reach the aircraft or primary work environment. Because of this, much emotional labor is performed *before* the start of the first flight.

MORE THAN JUST A "LOOK": CONTEMPORARY MANIFESTATIONS OF RACIALIZED EXPERIENCES

The idea that the position of pilot is one occupied and appropriate for white males serves as a backdrop for the experiences of white women and people of color throughout the airline industry. Pilots are highly educated and trained and many have prior military experience. As this position is one that carries a level of prestige and power, African American pilots become "noticed" by passengers and co-workers alike. Thus, the idea of hypervisibility becomes an aspect of the job that these pilots have to contend with in their daily interactions, and many note the contradictions that occur when they are simultaneously hypervisible and marginally invisible.[8] These experiences are evocative of the connection between the racialized nature of an industry and the normative structures that contribute to the maintenance of these institutional norms. One major response from these pilots pertaining to experiences in the industry deals directly with hypervisibility as insinuated through "looks" and the direct connection to the larger ideology of black positionality as one not belonging in the front of the aircraft. This contemporary method of racist expression is one that is subtle and often unspoken. Take the following example of Tina, a black female copilot, as she describes what the average day is like for her:

> You know I really used to want to conform for the business side of this and the people I have to work with, but I work in this environment and I am so conscious about how I look because I'm walking through the terminal and everybody stares at me. So I don't want them to stare at me any more than necessary (laughs). I get the big-eyed look. I get the head like *The Exorcist*. The funny thing is I don't even notice it anymore. When my co-workers come and walk with me they constantly tell me. I know it's there, but they think it's funny and they really, really see it. They tell me about all these looks I keep getting. I usually walk through the airport with my head down so that I don't have to make eye contact. When I do look at people, some smile, but most don't know what to do.

In Tina's words, African Americans have and maintain an awareness that they are seen as "different" and not fitting well with preconceived, stereotypical images of what represents airline pilots. Though African American pilots have this idea of their difference, it is largely the result of white insistence that they somehow do not belong in the uniform, not to mention the flight deck. Though largely downplayed in significance by whites, these expressive looks have an emotional consequence for the African Americans experiencing them. In the above quote, this female pilot notes that she now walks through the airport with her head down so that she does not have to meet the stares of those around her. The frequency of these stares has caused many of these pilots to create ways to maneuver their environment, one that has a consequence—here the consequence is a loss of confidence. For many, understanding the notion of emotional labor as one performed within the context of jobs should also note those aspects of emotional labor resulting from unspoken experiences. As many in the mainstream public may connect the attention given by African Americans to "looks" as racial paranoia, those African Americans interviewed here understood those not-so-innocent looks to be driven by racial identity.

Though most all of the pilots in this project shared experiences with stares, they often note that they were left wondering *why* these stares occur. Many perceive it to be based on gender, while others note race, gender, and age. Important in this idea is that there is involved a level of conscious thought that takes place on behalf of these pilots that occurs outside of those other significant aspects of job performance. In context, the time and energy given to analyze these experiences also contribute to the amount of emotional labor these pilots perform. Lisa, a female pilot, shares her experiences with looks in the following manner:

> For the most part you just kind of deal with it and after a while it becomes second nature . . . you go, "Yeah, you're looking . . . I get it." I remember coming into Pittsburgh with my uniform on and it was like, oh my God, I landed from Mars . . . I mean everybody was staring (laughs). I mean I understand why everybody is staring. It's like, oh my God, she's a pilot—she's black—she looks so young. Or, she's a woman . . . I mean, you know it still gets to you even after a while.

Here, she confirms the idea of an African American pilot as anomaly in the idea that she "landed from Mars." As she discusses the looks she gets from passengers, she easily references her gender, race, and age, which collectively create a complex experience. Though she does not explicitly state a singular reason people are staring, she does note that it becomes "second nature" to deal with these pervasive and unspoken methods of exclusion. Even unspoken, many of these pilots not only designate these looks as experiences important in their daily interactions but they also designate meaning to these interactions. Take, for instance, another example of "the look" as expressed by a male pilot.

> I do get funny looks, and when I do they are obvious. It's not like a glance or a slight double take. The hatred sets in, so I would say that out of maybe every hundred people I see, one of them can't stop staring at me with a frown on their face like, "What the hell is that?" They'll stare for minutes and minutes. You know how people usually will look away when you catch them staring? Well, they are so into their stare that it takes them a few moments to realize that you have caught them staring at you.

In this account, more detail is provided concerning the perceived meaning behind the stares that he receives. The long-standing notion that there are no significant meanings to a look is indeed untrue to these black pilots. For them, they understand that these stares are an implicit method used to insinuate that they do not belong in this particular space. Though often attributed to paranoia, these African American pilots have conceptually described and argued that there are meanings as well as feelings conveyed in a look. The idea that stares are a covert method of exclusion is coupled with the idea that they are indeed noticed in a way their white counterparts are not. Note, too, that the first excerpt provided by the female pilot notes that not only do her co-workers "see it, [but they also find it] funny." The notion that these stares are somehow humorous involves a level of power on behalf of her co-workers, as they can find humor in experiences deemed very uncomfortable for her. This also suggests that it is largely downplayed and deemed insignificant to those whites around her. The recollections of these pilots provide an implicit understanding that though largely seen by outsiders as insignificant experiences, they deserve more discussion.

Because words are not exchanged in these interactions, it is possible that many outsiders will assume that the analyses provided by these pilots are mere imagination, ones they themselves have provided meaning to. Be that as it may, these interactions carry both meaning and consequences for these pilots. While many have the privilege for looks to go unnoticed and analyzed, these pilots note that they do not have this particular luxury, as it is a large aspect of their job. "The look of hatred," as named by many pilots, can occur in organizations where groups are only represented in token numbers. Rosabeth Moss Kanter, in her discussion of women underrepresented in organizations, notes that visibility and invisibility of women in organizations means automatic notice or the inability to remain anonymous; much evaluation of their performance is based on salient characteristics and not on how the job was actually performed. Therefore, underrepresented women and men face the dilemma of having their identity recognized while their accomplishments are unnoticed.[9] Many minority group members in situations where they are underrepresented hold a collective understanding of what is represented in a "look." Too, there is a knowledge held by African Americans that the notion that a look contains any implicit meaning is denounced by more mainstream society, leaving them to develop a system of distinguishing the unspoken yet recognizable meaning of "looks." When asked to develop the idea of how meaning is derived from looks, one pilot, Marcus, eloquently states:

> You can tell when a person sees you and likes you. I think, you know, you can tell when a person is pleasantly pleased by what they're looking at.
> [Give me an example.]
> So I was standing by the door and I would greet people and kind of take a look and see what's going on or who's coming on. And it's normally when folks are already on the plane and they're getting in their seats and there's a line that's backed up, backed up into the jet way. And they're about the second or third or fourth person about to get on the plane, and then they notice me. And they notice my stripes. And it tends to be a woman, a white woman, and it tends to be an older woman. And she will look at me—she's like, wait a minute. What the fuck? And it hits them; it's like . . . oh shit! He's flying me today. But they won't say anything . . . Sometimes they do, but many won't. They will look at me, I have my uniform on, I have my ID on, I have my badge on and it's right in front of them and they're reading it. It's like they want to burn a hole through my ID so I can't fly, and then I'll look at them, and they'll look away. They don't want to make direct eye contact with me . . . And if I look away and I keep half an eye on them, they're right back to checking me out . . . They're judging me from the top down. And I get that as a captain all the time. And the minute I look at them to engage them, "Welcome aboard, how are you?"—they look away. So it's like they don't want to engage me

directly but they want to judge me when my back is turned or I'm looking away or whatever. You can tell when there's *contempt*.

This captain, with many years of experience, talks about the methods he uses to distinguish looks received from passengers. The idea of contempt, or what many other participants described as disgust, is something these African American pilots have a great awareness of. As with those accounts mentioned earlier, most note that one method of differentiating meanings in looks involve the concurrent facial expressions. As noted in these above accounts, many of these looks are accompanied by frowns and are considered "hate stares."[10] Additionally, these stares are connected to white backstage behavior, and clearly, whites in these examples are shocked into putting now-backstage racism into frontstage behavior.[11]

The idea that there is more to a "look" than meets the uninitiated eye is indeed important in our understandings of contemporary racial experiences. Recognizing the notion that the nature of oppression and exclusion have changed to more covert and subtle mechanisms than in the pre-1960s era is important here. The idea of racial change often allows these racist practices to be dismissed, and they are difficult for those not experiencing this to recognize. It also allows those in more privileged racial and gendered positions within occupations to maintain that privilege—to dismiss the additional emotional labor connected to these seemingly small, yet cumulative, events. Looking deeper, the reality of race and racism for these black pilots is reaffirmed in these white, subtle emotional expressions and their hypervisibility. Deeply examining what these pilots experience through covert racism has meaning for the larger profession and those that occupy these positions. Most significantly, these small events can add additional emotional labor to an occupation already emotionally taxing.

OCCUPATIONAL STEREOTYPES AND RACIAL UNIFORMS

Much of this suggests that not only is the position of pilot continuously racialized as a white profession but also that the uniform itself represents whiteness. For example, Ronald, a senior captain with over twenty years of experience, notes:

> Well, there are those people who will see you in uniform and want to give you their bags if you are standing anywhere near the front of the airport. The thing that I notice the most is whenever I am in uniform and near the traveling public, people will tend to look, especially white males, will tend to look you up and down. It becomes kind of obvious that they're asking the question, "What is he doing in a uniform?"

Moreover, another senior pilot commented:

> At the hotel, I can be standing there waiting for the van to take us to the airport
> and passengers have come up and dropped their bags at my feet on more than
> one occasion. I was flying with a black captain and we were waiting in the
> lobby, in full uniform, and a white guy walked up to him and said, "Can you
> get my cab for me?" The captain looked at him and said, "The only thing we
> know how to do is fly airplanes." The man said, "I understand that, but can
> you get my cab for me?" He just couldn't get it through his mind that he was
> talking to a pilot.

Contemporary racism relies heavily on the mechanism of refurbished ideas of African American inferiority. Though these pilots are men and women in uniform, African American pilots find themselves in the situation of having to deal largely with the perceptions of others—their pilot's uniform becomes a skycap's, a doorman's, or the cleaning crew uniform. Thus, most become aware that many in the white traveling public see them as not fitting the appropriate icon of what constitutes an airline pilot. One recurring theme in my interviews was that often interactions with passengers extended beyond "looks" and included the spoken idea that African Americans should be in a position of servitude or low-wage service work. Several interviewees mentioned the commonality that they were often given luggage as though they are baggage handlers. For instance, when discussing her experiences in uniform, one female pilot commented: "On a flight, there was this one particular time that I was standing at the door with my uniform on and this passenger came over to me as though I was the cleaner. I kinda went off, in a professional way, and I reiterated to her that I was the pilot. I mean, it happens sometimes. *They just don't see us.*"

The gendered racism and racial narratives faced by African Americans in this industry is catapulted to the forefront through the representation of the uniform. Easily recognizable, with stripes, hat, and flight bags, African American men and women in uniform are subjugated to lower-level positions, denying them simultaneously of their skill and hard work. These men and women wear what Robert Park (1928) called a "racial uniform," or the racial hallmark, made up of physical traits, that causes judgment and evaluation based on color. Implicitly, race and gender serve as a uniform, providing stereotypical notions, which are quickly referenced, of what it means to be a black man or woman on the aircraft. These racial uniforms are gendered and can trump the very common and recognizable uniform of the pilot instantly.[12] Besides passengers approaching African American workers with a case of "mistaken identity," it is an altogether different situation when this same behavior is mimicked by those that are employed by the airline industry. As one female pilot notes, "I often have to point out my name under *pilots* because they often assume I am a flight attendant."

There are racialized factors at play in these cases, factors associated with underlying assumptions of black positions and skill sets. Outside of what it means for those African American pilots, the racialization of what constitutes appropriateness for the position of pilot is also evident here. In these encounters, the uniform and position represent whiteness, and in this representation, the underlying assumption is that African Americans are not granted full participation or recognition in this role. Also, the racialization of black males and females ensures that they are "mistaken" for those in low-skilled positions and are challenged with the position to counter those ideologies. In fact, one aspect of understanding these subtle interactions is the idea that in many contemporary settings, African Americans often "meet negative beliefs about and interpretations of their abilities, values, and orientations."[13] The removal of power, position, and recognition of pilot is but one example that these African Americans face in their daily interactions on the job. Because there is inherent privilege associated with not having to notice the racialized experiences of others, these black pilots often find themselves faced with the duality of experiencing racism firsthand while also having to teach others that it continues to exist.

Here, it is important to note that though black flight crews are hypervisible to the traveling public, their white colleagues often downplay the significance of these looks and other subtle experiences. In these cases, African Americans use these experiences as a method of "teaching" whites about their experiences. For instance, Tony used such a discussion as an opportunity to show his white copilot just how much things remain the same for African Americans in this industry:

> I was flying with an older white captain that wanted to have a racial discussion on how things have changed and are better for African Americans . . . He kept saying, "Don't you see the difference?" I was thinking, I'm not going to say anything, but I did say, "I'm going to ask you to do me a favor. Walk behind me through the terminal when we get back to the airport." And he's like, "Huh?" "Just walk behind me, just a few feet behind me, and see the way other people look at me." And then we walked toward our other plane, we got on our other plane and I'm like, "Did you see anything?" And he couldn't believe it. Because he could see from an older black person who had watched me and said, "Oh my God. I've never seen one before!" So it went from an old black person saying, "Oh my God, I never seen one before, *thank you*, Lord" to an older white person that said, "Oh my God, I hope they're not flying my plane." I had to tell him, you get that; you get those reactions—and sometimes it's just within the eyes, I mean, their eyes will lock on you and they will express it through their eyes, that contempt of, you know, "he doesn't know what he's doing."

Because many of the African Americans believe whites do not "see" racism from their perspective, this pilot used an opportunity to counter the broadly held idea that African Americans no longer encounter any racial issues. This long-standing belief that "racism is dead" is one that is found in the continual denial of black experiences, one that seeks to maintain white innocence and reduce racist encounters to a few "bad" individuals. Never included in this is that these bad individuals are encountered on a regular basis or the fact that these individuals are a part of the outer, more inclusive society that allows for the constant reproduction of racist ideology through a variety of venues. Understanding that racism is systemic allows a deeper connection between the racial experiences of African Americans, white expectations about black pilots, and the institutionalization of racism within the aviation industry. These organizational characteristics were created *within* a racist system. As I move on to the ways in which African American pilots experience invisibility, keep in mind that these encounters in the terminal (and even before) begin before any work is to actually take place, thereby contributing to the overall amount of emotional labor to be performed.

THE EMOTIONS OF INVISIBILITY

In the previous section, I examined the hypervisibility African American pilots experience in their initial interactions with passengers and co-workers. Though many of these interactions are unspoken, they nonetheless involve a level of emotional labor that should be recognized. As the industry seeks to provide good customer service and safety, aspects of social identity also contribute to the performance of emotional labor that is outside of this context of required work. In this section, I introduce the subtle and nuanced interactions that take place with white co-workers. Continuing with the idea of the subtleties of racialized interactions, I now turn to the other side of visibility, what many of these pilots describe as "invisibility." Take, for instance, the following account of a senior pilot:

> I guess I have this technique of fading in the background and so people don't realize I am there. I was in the crew room one day and the conversation was on rolling cigarettes. This one guy says, "Well, you need to nigger-lip it." I was there, and I glanced back at one of the other guys and he was trying to tell him not to say that. I didn't react. I think it was an embarrassing moment for him. I think they were expecting me to make some equal opportunity protest or some shit like that but I said nothing about it.

In this account, there is a spatial reality of race and racism. Keep in mind that this encounter occurred in a common room used by multiple crew members. To examine this idea from the perspective of the African American pilot, he notes that people are often unaware of his presence (or possibly they simply ignore his presence). For many in this industry those things associated with being a pilot are also associated with whiteness, even by co-workers. The comfort to speak and engage in behaviors that are often considered to occur in settings that are more private indicates the long-standing notion that this occupation is one that is occupied and maintained for whites, specifically white males. As a method of maintaining white superiority, many whites engaged in blatant language against African Americans. The flight deck as well as crew rooms and other areas associated with being a pilot serve as a safe space for these white pilots—a space where they are free to use racist language. For this pilot and other African American pilots, because they are in an industry dominated by white males, they have to contend with the fact that a great deal of these spaces are unsafe (and even sometimes hostile) spaces in which they are not free to counter many of these racist interactions. As this industry is spatially and culturally white, norms, ideologies, and customs that involve racist narratives and stereotypes are salient activities in this environment. To understand emotional labor in this case, we have to understand the possible outcomes for the black pilot if he had called them on their racist language.

When on the aircraft, the idea of being invisible, specifically when in positions of authority, is often manifest in a number of ways. Co-workers often reiterate the perception that African Americans do not belong on the aircraft in a way that suggests that they do not fear any verbal or physical backlash. As the hierarchy in the flight deck is well established, one captain laughs and mentions, "This one guy who was flying as my copilot tried to confront me by saying, 'So you think you're in charge?' I don't know what his problem was, but he wasn't too bright. Most people I fly with understand the *power relationships* and they know not to cross that line."

This first officer mockingly stating, "So you think you're in charge?," is indicative of how he views not only the hierarchy on the aircraft but also of his larger views of social power dynamics. For various reasons, this first officer found it appropriate and necessary to outright challenge the authority of the captain while insinuating how he disregards his power. This is also a method that reaffirms the idea of the flight deck as a space that remains largely as a white space. The senior pilot in this narrative notes that this was one of several instances in which his authority was challenged, further noting that "this one time, I had one of my first officers use the 'n' word and he thought he was going to get a reaction out of me but I didn't react." Within the confines of the flight deck, many of these African Americans understand that it is not the appropriate space to react, and so do the many white actors who take part in this blatantly racist behavior. Thus, we have to consider how this weighs heavily on the part of the recipient while also understanding the emotional process of the actor. Consider also the following example from Anthony:

Just before the plane closes, one of the agents from the gate will come down and bring the final paperwork: Tell us how many people we have on board, that kind of stuff. Normally, their job is to give it to the captain, ask the captain if he needs anything, wants anything, if it's okay to close the door. Heard from a number of black captains that the same thing happens to them . . . They are sitting in the left seat [captain's seat], they'll give it [the paperwork] to the white first officer. "Is there anything else you need?" And they'll hand it to them. They try to get approval from the white first officer to close the door, and they have to get stopped.

Being a former commanding officer, retired commanding officer, I will very quickly and very easily get into that aristocratic "I'm in charge" mode . . . But that natural way of thinking; you know . . . white is right, brown stick around, black get back mentality—it's just natural because they were raised with it. So, when you call them on it, they have to think twice. Like I just mentioned when the agent tries to avoid that black captain by giving the paperwork to the white first officer . . . You know your left from your right; you know the difference between three and four, so there is no doubt in your mind which one of these shoulders has four stripes. *And you do this every day; you hand the paperwork to the captain every day.* The only difference in this cockpit today is the guy with four stripes has a sun tan.

Largely resulting from a history of systematic exclusion, the airline industry, specifically the flight deck, has developed as a white space—a space in which whites, especially white males, created and continue to maintain the ideological and normative frameworks of who belongs and doesn't belong in the cockpit. As can be seen, white co-workers and passengers alike reiterate this overarching ideology. Note here, too, the extended and cumulative effects of racial experiences occurring for these flight crews. Many of these racialized experiences occur before the start of the workday and continue long after the day ends. Racism to those experiencing it is a never-ending story of sorts, one that greets them when they step outside and is not shut off when the workday begins and ends. By examining their collective experiences in the workplace, we can explicate the mechanisms of systemic racism and the overarching white framing that facilitate the reproduction of racism in this institutional setting. Systemic racism has produced (and maintained) a larger societal system that in many ways normalizes racism and racist encounters. That racism has become normative can be found in the denouncing of its continued existence. This is somewhat evident in negative reactions of whites to only minimal social change in the airline industry and also normalizes the expectation held by many blacks that they will indeed encounter racial affronts at one point or another while at work.

The actions of white actors should also be discussed as it pertains to the labor performed by African American flight crews. In these accounts, whites serve as usurpers of black authority, skills, and emotional expressions. Given the process of engaging feeling and performing emotional labor, whites in this environment feel free to engage in inappropriate behaviors suggesting that they have a freedom to imply the old familiar adage of African Americans in lower-status positions. In this, whites often attempt to remove the power given to African Americans in rather collective attempts to reaffirm white privilege and white space.

Through these interactions, both spoken and unspoken, the spatial reality of the flight deck as a white space serves the larger purpose of reaffirming the normative expectations of power, privilege, and emotional expressions. Through their dealings with whites on the aircraft as well as in their daily lives, African Americans have had to undergo the process of learning to not only manage their own emotions but have also learned through systemic racism and white framing how to effectively manage the racist emotions of others.

LABOR COSTS: WAGES OF EMOTIONAL LABOR

For the most part, African Americans expend considerable emotional energy to maneuver their social worlds—one outside of work that recognizes and acts on their racial identity, and another at work that reiterates their position as outsiders. One large aspect of emotional labor is to produce in others a particular feeling while also being protective of self. Missing from much of the literature is the idea that interlocking identities add an entirely new dimension to emotional labor—one that has severe consequences when performed by African Americans in this context. The consequences to self are often staggering.

Outside of performing this emotion work pertaining to visibility, African Americans also face and deal with larger, more blatant racist practices of exclusion. In many respects, African American pilots often deal with the blatant idea that they do not belong or "fit," as many describe. Whites in the workplace use various tactics to reaffirm the cockpit and the position of pilot as one reserved for whites only. From training to actual job performance, these black pilots contend with how passengers interact with them as well as how fellow crew reaffirm their positions as one that whites are only fully capable of performing.

EARLY ACCOUNTS OF WHITE NORMATIVITY: TRAINING EXPERIENCES OF BLACK FLIGHT CREWS

The idea of the aircraft as a white space starts well before being hired for an airline, and many of these black pilots note that even their experiences with training were emotionally trying. The process of emotional labor involved in expressions of exclusion aimed at their intellect and skill evokes frustration, anger, and disappointment. Even so, these flight crews maintain awareness that because of their racial identity and the long-standing negative stereotypes of black Americans, emotional expressions of most sorts are seen as inappropriate. Consider the following example of Martin, a pilot in his early thirties, as he recounts his experiences in training to become a commercial pilot. Entering the industry after graduating college and interning for a regional carrier, Martin noted the overall exclusive picture he observed when he entered his first training class. He states,

> When I graduated from college, I was an intern for a regional carrier; one of the first interns from a historically black college, and there was also another black guy from my school. I was at the training center at the airport. Basically, I was responsible for learning all the intricacies of training and flying aircraft. Now, being an intern, I was guaranteed an interview with this regional carrier, and I was also given the opportunity to take a training class with all of the pilots. Keep in mind that I am an intern and everyone in the class was already pilots. I was the first one in our group to go through the training class. There were only four black people, including myself, in the building. There was a brother that worked there and two sistas that worked in scheduling. Other than that, it was no black people. There were no Asians, and there were very few females.

Many African Americans are familiar with the experience of being represented in token numbers in many predominantly white occupations. This experience, seemingly minor, still carries a tacit understanding and expectations for interactions. Being on display, with a lack of any significant support, can indeed produce an unsettling emotional experience. As Martin continues his discussion of the training experience, he states,

> There was a guy named Dale that was over the classroom and he kept all of the books. Well, when they told me it was time to go to training, they told me to just show up to class and I would get everything I needed in there. Well, when I get to class, all the pilots had books and training materials and [Dale] didn't give me any. So I thought maybe they just want me to sit here, but I took notes and all that. I'm trying to follow as best I can but I don't have any books. Well, the day before the final exam for the class, the guy Dale comes up and says that "your internship success is based on how you do on this exam." I said, "Dale, I don't have any books and I haven't had any for the entire class." So he says, "Here you go."
>
> Overnight I studied all night long and I didn't go to sleep at all, and I got up and took my exam. I passed. He was clearly upset that I passed. The other interns got their materials before so that they could study . . . I was interning so there wasn't a whole lot I could say. I did tell some people but nothing happened. To me it was clearly racist.
>
> [What do you mean he was clearly upset? How was he upset?]

> When the instructors came back with the tests, they did say we had one failure and everybody thought it was me but it was a pilot who was working there had failed. The look on [Dale's] face; he did not hide it. He was disappointed that it wasn't me who had failed. I'm sure he wanted the chance to say, "See, we wasted our time bringing this black kid in here."

Though never explicitly stated to Martin that his experiences were based on his racial identity, Martin, a new intern for an airline, spent considerable time and energy—energy that could have been used for more productive endeavors—pondering the behaviors of those around him. To have the emotional experience and perception that he was expected to fail, along with the notion that the instructor wanted the chance to say, "See, we wasted our time bringing this black kid in here," is an all-consuming process—one that implicitly gives Martin the feeling that this environment is not for him. Even as Martin discusses his experience in the classroom during training, he notes that this process of exclusion did not start there; exclusion started before he even entered the classroom.

> Even before then, our first day there was one other black intern and he was in the chief pilot's office in the terminal. We both showed up the night before the first day and we got an email from this guy stating that orientation started promptly at 8 o'clock. Well, we got up that morning and were both driving over. When we got to the parking lot, the *one* black guy that worked there, he came running outside. He said, "All the Caucasians are already there!" And we were like, "It's 7:45, we're fifteen minutes early." "NO, the orientation started at 7!" Luckily, the other guy had printed out the email and that saved us. They sent all the other interns an email stating that it started at 7. We had to show the email that was sent to us. Now, the only conclusion I can draw from that was that it was racially motivated. They tried to make it look like we couldn't show up on time.

In this account, there are several examples of one method often used by whites to reiterate the ideas of white space and black inferiority—sabotage. The first example can be seen in the fact that the necessary training materials that would help to ensure success were not given to Martin in a timely fashion. In this way, it was assumed that the flight instructor would provide those materials, and when this was mentioned by Martin, a simple "Here you go" was provided. Moreover, the correct time to report for training was not provided to the two black males in this particular orientation class. In this account, it is clear that this pilot had given these facts considerable thought, as referenced by his idea that he could not help but think these incidences were racially motivated. There is much that can be gained from this excerpt. To sabotage their possible progress in this program is but one aspect of this interaction. But regardless of the trainer's motivation, his actions produced a sabotage that would likely reaffirm to all others involved the long-standing stereotype of black inferiority (blacks are lazy, unreliable, and will not show up on time). Indeed, these stereotypes are not new creations, but deeply embedded, shared notions of black pathology, found even in a period of color blindness and race neutrality.[14]

As this conversation continued, Martin noted that they made a complaint, but nothing ever happened, which suggests that there is no punishment for discriminatory treatment and no purpose of speaking up against it. In many respects, the existence of both perspectives suggests that those things associated with flying—from training to the actual job—are normative structures maintaining these white spaces. Also included in this account is the idea that Martin had a racial awareness of being that was indeed only one of a "handful" of African Americans at this particular location. The idea of being racially aware, specifically in terms of racial diversity or lack thereof, is one that most African Americans note in terms of their surroundings. It can serve as an indication that a level of preparedness is involved when in an environment deemed a white (unsafe) space. Too, because race was never explicitly stated, Martin quickly understood that the burden of proof would fall on him—how could he prove to others in management, who were overwhelmingly white, that the incidents he experienced in training were based on race? Martin carried this knowledge, and he carried this burden alone. One would have to imagine the emotional labor associated with returning to an environment each day in which you are methodically excluded.

In another example of the various methods used during training, Rob notes his experiences when he was initially hired by National Freight, a worldwide freight carrier, and his experience with being given multiple instructors in a short amount of time. Also, in this particular case, training materials were provided sparingly:

> I went through ground school, finished top of the class, and got ready to go into what they call FTD, flight training devices, where you go through a mockery of what you're going to do in the actual simulator, and went through four instructors—actually two instructors during that period—and I was doing things exactly from chapter 3 in the normal procedures of the book, and the emergency procedures in chapter 2, but they would say, "You're going too fast." Or, "You're going too slow." And I said, "Would you demonstrate for me?" And it got to the point where I was reluctant to speak back. But when I made up my mind, like this ain't making sense, I'm doing exactly what the book says on page 13 from the top to the bottom; I'd memorize it . . . So that guy would leave and I would get a new one and he says, "That's not the way you do it!" So, well, "Bobby showed me this is how you do it." He says, "That's not the way you do it." And every time they do that they write it on paper and they have these long dissertations. And I kept thinking I know I can do this, cause what I didn't mention before is I was already rated on the 737. I'd won a scholarship earlier and walked into a national airline training course

and got a captain's check out of them. So I know I'm capable of absorbing and learning . . . What am I doing wrong?[15]

Much like the experiences of Martin, Rob has a tacit knowledge that he is being sabotaged. In this account, he begins to question his skill set as he asks himself what he is doing wrong. This experience, emotionally draining as it may be, is one that Rob experiences singly. Making the statement that he spoke up initially, he also understands the authority of the flight instructors, yet he knows he is amply qualified to fly this aircraft. As Rob continues his training, he came to the conclusion that his experiences were based on his racial identity.

> I go back in it the next day, and I remember the day I got my uniform; I tried it on, looked at myself in the mirror with it, and knew I would never wear that uniform at work. I didn't fit their culture, I didn't fit the thinking . . . So I went to the next level in the simulator, did the same thing, and Stan was the last instructor, and I stood up to him, I said, "Something ain't right. You guys are not, you know, I'm doing this exactly"—and then they put me with Chris. Chris, the guy that actually designed the interior of [one of the large aircraft] . . . And, I remember it . . . there was a board as long as this wall [Rob points to the back wall of the library] and I did all of them . . . the 727 QF, the 727-100, 727-200, and the 727-300 . . . I did every system on that board . . . the electrical systems, the hydraulic systems on each airplane.
> And he said, "I don't know what your problem is." I said, "It ain't me, it's them!" And at that time you didn't point fingers at someone, tell somebody else how to train you. And they brought me to the fleet manager of the airplane, and he yelled at me, and I told him, "You know what, whatever it's going to take" . . . So they gave me another training session, then I went in for the check ride, the check ride was being given by a white female . . . I walked into the sim [simulator] and was getting everything ready, but something was broken. I wrote it up in the log book, and simulated calling maintenance to come and fix it, and he walked in and said, "We don't do it that way at National Freight; your check ride is over with!" And about an hour and a half later, I was sitting in a boardroom signing resignation papers, and my job was done. The thing is I already knew this . . . The airlines had to start tiptoeing a little better and *refining their racism* so they were in a better position . . . You know, put you in difficult situations where you're destined to fail. Multiple instructors in a short period of time. It's also a recipe for disaster, you know, set him up to fail . . . Little underhanded things like that.

In this account, there is an awareness of the various methods used to influence outcomes in training sessions. For instance, in his discussion of being hired by National Freight, Rob noted that he knew he would never wear his uniform in a full work setting. In noting that he would never fit their culture or way of thinking, this captain understood that there were aspects of his identity that were different from others—his identity as an African

American male. Also important in his discussion is the fact that eventually Rob decided to speak out against things he perceived to be wrong, but there was a negative consequence; he soon signed his resignation papers. Both Martin and Rob, in their different yet similar experiences, carried a comprehension of the difficulties they could possibly face in these environments, indicating that the difficulties they faced were not new, suggesting that both were familiar with these methods. Indeed, Rob even states his awareness that this sabotage and the difficulty to prove that his experiences are based on race is simply a new, improved, and refined way of being racist.

Many of these methods used by instructors and those in management are underhanded and subtle ways to sabotage those in training. This process of "weeding out" potential black pilots during training is also an added dimension of maintaining white spaces and the emotional labor done by African Americans in this industry. To place this in better context, consider the following example, provided by a young male pilot with less than ten years of commercial flying experience. This example takes place as he prepares to enter a new company where experiences with race were more blatant:

> During the training, we had an instructor for the ground school, we had six weeks of ground school in Tulsa, and then we went to Atlanta where we used the simulators of another airline, and there was myself and my partner who was also black. [The instructor] pretty much told us, point blank, he didn't think we'd do a good job because we were black.
> [What did he say?]
> That. Pretty much.
> The thing is we started with him, we met on day one, we couldn't quite read him because what we do is we brief about an hour before we do a session . . . So day one he's going over stuff that is really basic and we didn't understand why he was breaking it down in such small bites, but he was the instructor, we were just listening, you know maybe he had some point he's building towards . . . But then, I'd say a week into this, my partner and I are in my room, and we're studying together, and [the instructor] me and asks if I wanted to have a beer . . . So we met him downstairs. He was already drunk; like wasted . . . And while we're sitting outside waiting he just says, "I want to clear something up; just cause I'm white and you're black, I hope this doesn't cause a problem." And my partner goes, "Oh, I'm black, really?" And he's like, "Yeah, yeah, you are," and he's drunk so he's not really getting the sarcasm, you know, and he's like "Yeah, I just don't want there to be any problems, I hope there's nothing wrong with that." I was like, "I don't understand why there would be a problem . . ." I was like, "Have you had a black student?" He was like, "Well, no, you guys are my first." And I was like, "Well, did you think this was going to be a problem having two black students?" And he was like "Well, honestly, yeah. I did. Nobody told me you guys were black. I saw you guys come out the elevator, I was like aw, shit; black guys! These guys aren't gonna know anything." So we're just kind of looking at him like, for real? And then he goes on to say, "It's crazy because I

thought you guys wouldn't know anything and that I was going to have to lower the bar to get you through . . . I didn't know black people could learn like that."

In this particular example, the flight instructor relied heavily on the age-old stereotypes and white framing of African Americans and their intellectual skill and abilities. One important aspect of this interaction is that the instructor felt comfortable sharing his opinions as though he believed not much would be said in return. The privilege found in the freedom to be vocal about prejudices in a period of stress to these young students indeed served as a sort of racial catharsis for this instructor. This instructor continues in his discussion of why he did not want there to be any problems. He noted that he and his close white friends sometimes use the "n" word as a joke to each other, but he doesn't mean it in a negative way. He did not want there to be a problem if it slipped out. In his disclaimer, he stated, "I am sure you use derogatory language when talking about whites sometimes." As I continued my conversation with this young pilot, he noted that he was in disbelief at the actions of the instructor and was also disappointed in his language. He notes, "Honestly, I was like, man, you know; I know white people think this but they never tell you. I was thinking, wow, this is honest." There is much to be said concerning the comfort and privilege provided to this instructor through the belief that he can speak freely in such a racist manner. By opening his statement with "I don't want there to be any problems," the white instructor used a very passive method of ensuring trouble would not erupt by attempting to remove any racist intent. If the African American pilots perceived prejudice, they would be reduced to being sensitive about race. After all, he didn't mean it. Stereotyping and prejudice are part of a much larger social scaffolding. This defense of white power and privilege comes at a direct cost to those African Americans in this industry and serves as a consistent reminder that they are not fully accepted as intellectual equals.[16] In the aforementioned racialized accounts, these African American flight crews suffer the emotional costs through the emotional labor of having to simultaneously balance their love of flying with the consequence of being black in an extremely white and sometimes hostile environment.

HOW DID YOU GET IN THAT SEAT?
THE EMOTIONAL LABOR OF EXCLUSION

Much of the discourse concerning African Americans in the airline industry is that they are incapable of being good pilots. The deflation that takes place during and after interactions such as those already mentioned is indicative to these pilots' understandings of what is to come. The idea that negative attitudes end once training is completed is something most of these black pilots understand to be untrue. Pilots of color realize that there is a normative discourse concerning black inferiority from a very old, white, racial frame, here as it pertains to flying airplanes. As whites have historically held these high positions on the aircraft, there is the consequence of white backlash toward these African American pilots. One such characteristic of white backlash is outright exclusion. One common method of exclusion mentioned by these African Americans comes through the failure of their co-workers to engage in conversation with them while at work. Many note sitting in the flight deck for hours with *no* conversation of any sort. Take the following example from Johnny as he discusses an experience with a co-worker.

> I got mad once the *first time* a captain didn't shake my hand. 'Cause I'd been here like two years and I pride myself on doing my job very well . . . And for him to just get up, get his stuff, no goodbye, no "Great job"—'cause you're kind of looking for that as a first officer, you're looking for some feedback . . . But to have someone just get up, walk out, no goodbye, I mean, one, it's rude, right, but two, it's borderline disrespectful and insulting on a certain level. So we can work together but you can't shake my hand?
>
> You're kind of in shock because the checklists are all done and I'll usually wait for the captain to leave so that I can make sure the cockpit is back where it needs to be for the next person. And I am sitting there looking at him, waiting and thinking, oh, okay, well he's just getting his luggage but he's coming right back . . . and then he has his luggage and is walking out into the jet way and I am thinking, did this motherfucker—wait [makes a loud grunting noise]—I can't believe this shit just happened! I can't believe this mother . . . just did that. So then you go through your stuff and you're just pissed off!

Here, we must imagine the difficulties and confines of the flight deck and what this means for these pilots. The idea that there will be cordial conversation along with mutual respect is not too much to ask for these pilots. More than that, it is this common social element of the job that African American pilots are excluded from.[17] In fact, this pilot had the expectation that at the end of a successful trip, a handshake would take place. Indicative here is the idea and desire of these pilots to be accepted and belong in the flight deck. Though a covert method of exclusion was used in this example, it was apparent to this first officer that he was not fully accepted by his colleague. This method of exclusion was a common one among these male pilots, and many first officers noted the commonality in the dismissive behavior of captains and first officers after flights have concluded. Again, this is indicative of the larger white racial framing of African Americans. Moreover, as the pilot mentions that he was "pissed," we have to consider that this experience remained with him for the remainder of the day.

Another detail that shapes pilots' experiences is questions concerning the amount of training and education they have received. For most, there is the awareness that in many cases, they have indeed received extensive training, even more so than their white counterparts. Even so, with these years of experience, many African American pilots are often questioned about their abilities from their fellow co-workers. As explained briefly by one pilot:

> I can remember when I first checked out as captain of a 737, I had a first officer practically quiz me on my background, and I was as kind as I could be. I made him ask the questions; I wouldn't give answers unless he asked questions. And when he realized I'd been through these different airlines and all these different experiences . . . I mean eating particularly anything and everything you could just to get through the day cause you had enough money to survive for that night, tomorrow night, maybe a hotel room, head back home, and that type of stuff and this guys going to quiz *me* on what I had to do to be a captain and be qualified . . . So what's your background? After he went over his whole litany of picking [on] me, he says he came right out of high school, straight through college, daddy paid the money and got him a job because he was one of the senior pilots here at the time. He had no idea all I had been through—flying on airplanes where I had to put my hat on the dash to keep the rainwater from shorting out the radios and such. And he has the *nerve* to question me and what I'm capable of.

The idea of being reinterviewed by peers was commonplace in this environment. In this, there is an inherent assumption that most blacks in the industry have received their positions not through skill but through affirmative action programs. Also the hierarchy of power relationships in the flight deck that usually come with a certain level of respect is not provided to this captain, as seen in the questioning of his qualifications. In this example, this young first officer feels it is both appropriate and necessary to question this senior captain on his abilities to fly the aircraft. The insinuation of black incapability reaffirms white space, and the creation of a different narrative of blacks undeservingly entering the industry has indeed become a normative aspect in this space.[18] This particular narrative, found through systemic perspectives that African Americans are provided racial, social, and economic "gifts" by whites in their allowance of black entry into the industry, both reaffirms a collective white narrative of general white goodness while also providing a collective understanding that whites are now victims of their own generosity. Thomas, a fairly junior pilot, stated aptly, "The stereotype is [that] you don't know how to handle an airplane. For some strange reason, somehow you slipped through the cracks and you got in this seat. It's not because you're talented and it's not because of all the experiences and skill you bring, but somehow you got in the seat." As noted throughout this chapter, these pilots also face the challenge of having their racialized experience validated by peers or those in management. A major aspect of this white-male space is that there is an overarching power dynamic that serves to hinder and silence the voices of people of color and their experiences with prejudices, stereotypes, and racist experiences. There are those individual

actors who perpetuate racist notions and ideologies, and most of these ideologies are found in the larger society in which they were created. Many of these
contemporary examples of exclusion are but refurbished mechanisms used
throughout history. Engaging in emotional labor, this pilot states that he "was
as kind as [he] could be," even while being openly challenged at work.

DON'T CLOSE THE BOARDING DOOR! PASSENGER
CONTRIBUTIONS TO THE MAINTENANCE OF WHITE SPACE

Implicit in this chapter is the idea that economic institutions and the emotions
that regulate them are a component of systemic racism and that the racial
framing of African Americans is an important element in the performance of
emotional labor. Too often, the daily experiences of African Americans in
professional and often white normative settings are viewed in a way that
suggests that the historical underpinnings of our racialized society ended
with the pivotal civil rights laws of the 1960s. Though the passage of these
laws was of extreme importance toward making racial progress, they in no
way suggest that contemporary experiences with racial discrimination and
oppression no longer exist. In many occupations in which people of color
remain underrepresented, the aspects of the white racial frame get passed
around through these social networks, thereby becoming a dominant frame
informing interactions with African American colleagues. As Joe Feagin
notes in his discussion of the white racial frame, there are several aspects that
are included in this dominant frame. The features of this frame include racial
stereotypes, racial narratives and interpretations, racial images, racialized
emotions, and inclinations to discriminatory action.[19] The stereotypes and
images of African Americans found in this frame supersede those interactions in which many of these racist beliefs and ideologies are disproven by
those successful African Americans with many years of experience in the
industry. For many whites, inside and outside of the airline industry, this
dominant frame continues to permit the dismissal of black experiences with
racial oppression as coincidence, perception, and overexaggeration. This is
done in a way that problematizes black voices as collective misrepresenta-
tions of whites and white racism. One consequence of this denial is that racial
oppression is allowed to persist and gender and racial inequality is reproduced within organizations. Indeed, this perpetual process of marginalization
in the workplace produces a cognitive dissonance that must be reconciled
through emotional labor.[20]

THE PAINFUL REALITY OF RACISM:
STORIES BY UNHEARD VOICES

As noted throughout this chapter, there is a cumulative aspect of working in an exclusive environment for these pilots. In this environment, negative experiences based on race and gender happen at a frequency that often leaves these pilots angry as they resolve disconnections between unequal treatment and the ability to have those claims heard from management and co-workers. Therefore, one main avenue in which emotional labor is necessary for these pilots is through the dissonance between notions of justice, freedom to perform their job, and white perceptions of their abilities. As such, a major source of the emotional labor performed by black pilots results from their experiences in the workplace being marginalized; experiences seen by whites as mere *perception* and therefore not real. In the workplace, the narrative of black inferiority in skill is coupled with those structural norms that validate white racism and sexism and reduce valid discriminatory claims to black paranoia. One such argument against the validity of experiencing racism or sexism in the workplace is the overarching idea that malicious intent must be involved.[21] Problematic in itself and an element of the white racial frame, these pilots countered the notion of perceived racism and responded angrily in return.[22] The reality of cumulative anger through unheard claims is clear in the following response from Anthony.[23]

Fuck it . . . Let me give you something candid . . . I flew the Beech 99 for an Express Airline. There's no flight attendant on a Beech 99 . . . People are getting on the airplane and I'm standing at the bottom of the steps. And people are getting on and they look at me kind of strange, but this white lady looks up and she sees the white captain sitting in the seat. So you see the pilot there, and I guess she's thinking, well, he's got to be the flight attendant. . . . So she gets on the plane, I get on the plane, and I close the door . . . and then I walk up to the front and climb into the front. [In an elevated voice] "OH NO! OH NO! I can't fly on this plane!" She gets out of the seat. "OH NO!" And she gets off the plane, you know, I had to let her off. And she went to agent. "What's *he* doing here, I'm not flying on this plane!"

[Thank you for sharing that experience with . . .]

Now, oh, I'm not finished, oh no! Fast forward about twenty years (Anthony pounds the table). I'm flying a Beech 1900 for an airline. We had a flight attendant. She's in the back and I'm getting another copy of the release, so I hop off to go grab it and bring it back to the plane. I come up the steps and the captain is in the cockpit and the flight attendant is by the door and I'm talking to her [the flight attendant], and this lady is basically scolding me for interfering—'cause I'm talking to her [the flight attendant] and I'm talking to the cockpit, giving him the information that he needs from me, and I'm answering her questions also. And this [white] woman, she's scolding me, telling me, "Don't follow them boys; them boys are busy up there!" As, you know, I'm a flight attendant, so I shouldn't be bothering them. So "Yes ma'am, yes ma'am," I'm saying to her. So finally, I'm getting into the cockpit. And I could hear her; I didn't dare look back. *"What the hell!"* It dawned on her; this young lady, who happened to be white, was the flight attendant, and the guy sitting to the left, who happened to be white, was the pilot, and the guy getting in the cockpit to the right, who happened to be black, was also a pilot. And it dawned on her. "What the hell!" You know, she had an epiphany. And we heard "Oh, shit!" She was moving so fast to get off! *Now I don't how much more blatant you want! Do you want some more?*

In this mainstream belief in the perception of racism, the suppression that racism is real and experienced is critical in the continuation of oppression.[24] One major aspect in the continuation of oppression is to reframe the methods and meanings attached to racial experiences as meaningless, thereby attempting to remove the validity of the experiences of people of color. This can be found in the revamped rhetoric of color-blind ideologies or the ideology that the painful *reality* of racism is a product of black minds—not of white racism.[25] This language, as an aspect of the white racial frame, allows and creates a situation in which those who openly complain of racism are the problem, not racism. In the above account, Anthony easily referenced those cases (and even offered more) in which there was a very public display based on his racial identity. Likely based on the long-standing stereotypes and imagery of African Americans as intellectually inferior, these passengers made the conscious decision to leave the aircraft. This was also done in a manner in which all those on the aircraft were involved. In the first encounter, the female passenger actually went to a supervisor to attempt to have the black pilot removed from the trip. The privilege here is one that has historically been granted whites; for many decades, African Americans were not allowed on the aircraft. Coupled with the overarching stereotypes of people of color, there is a tacit level of fear on behalf of the many whites that "see" an African American in the flight deck of their airplane. Even in these blatant accounts, the underlying yet visible emotional pressure and pain placed on these pilots must be considered as a major component of their daily work interactions.

These public acts of deplaning are an act that also reaffirms the flight deck and the position of captain as a white space and white occupation. The normality and belief that certain segments of the aircraft are inappropriate for people of color is one that goes beyond co-worker interactions but also involves the overarching belief of passengers. These racially arrogant actions suggest that many in the traveling public as well as many of those working for the airline think that the flight deck is somehow marked "for whites only." Moreover, the accounts of passenger interactions with black flight crew members go beyond a few racial stereotypes and include a level of arrogance and power to disrupt work and well-being without a concern that the police will be called. This power and arrogance and the ensuing emotional backlash faced by black flight crews are a part of a structural (white) worldview in which racist expressions are not only acceptable but also a privilege. Though women and men of color have made great strides in accessing the flight deck, "in a racist society, members of racial ethnic groups are not readily rewarded or appreciated for memorable actions. Instead, negative stereotypes of target groups persist even in the face of contradictory evidence."[26] Moreover, the connections between notions of color blindness and institutionally discriminatory practices leave many African American pilots to experience these hostile acts alone or with other African Americans.

Another young male pilot noted an experience he had with a passenger and his (in)ability to fly the plane:

> For a second example, I was in Oklahoma and we were standing at the gate, waiting on the airplane to arrive so that we could get on the plane, load the passengers up, and fly to Houston.[27] Well, as the airplane was pulling up, a [white] woman walks up to me and she says, "Are you one of the pilots?" And I said, "Yes, ma'am, I am." She said, "I'm really, really scared." I said, "You don't have to be scared. Everything will be fine and the airplane is very safe. We'll get you to Houston and it will be a really quick flight; about an hour and a half at the most." She said, "Oh, it's not that; you see, I saw this movie and that is why I'm scared." So, I'm thinking that maybe she saw a movie where the airplane crashed or something. She said, "It was this movie and the airplane was goin' up and down and in circles and the pilot was smoking weed and the pilot was a rapper." Then I said, "Oh, you talkin' about *Soul Plane*? So, you think that all black pilots smoke weed and are goin' to have the plane going up and down and in circles and we just gonna run this ghetto airline? You think that is going to be your flying experience on this national airline?"

In the second account, the interlocking systems of gender and race are apparent in this female passenger's imagery and ideology of the black male as a rapper and drug user. As this pilot engages in emotional labor by trying to comfort the fears of this passenger, he realizes that her fears are of him—not flying. She relies heavily on white-framed negative stereotypes purported through the mainstream media and feels comfortable discussing this negative ideology with the pilot involved in a public space. Her open use of these stereotypical imageries is a method of reifying white supremacy in this context. This female passenger also removes from this pilot his hard-won position on the aircraft and his fundamental right for this respectable position. Moreover, in this attempted subjugation of his position and authority, the female passenger openly connects black male bodies with fear—fear in his incapability to safely operate the aircraft as well as fear associated with larger stereotypes of black males. Due to systemic racism and a continual framing of the industry as one that white males are more apt to perform, there are tremendous emotional costs for pilots of color, as seen in his response to the passenger. These examples illustrate the ideology that blacks somehow do not belong in these environments, and this racist reality is largely supported in the normative structures that continue to encourage these interactions between black flight crews and their co-workers and passengers. To engage in emotional labor for these crew members is beyond the scope of what is to be expected during the course of a "normal" workday, but it suggests that emotional labor cannot be removed from the context in which it operates.

What has been shown through these racialized interactions with co-workers and passengers is the larger racial ideology and racialized discourse on what constitutes a pilot. Implicit, too, in this are the positive notions of the skills and intellect of whites. One significant consequence of these beliefs is the reality of tacit negative stereotypical views of African American pilots and their ability to fly airplanes. In the cases provided previously, there is an overarching racialization of African Americans and their stratified positions both on and off the aircraft. This is an important dimension of emotional labor and emotion management. There is not only a spatial reality that should be included in this theory but also one that factors in the larger societal reality of racial oppression.

WHY ARE YOU HERE? NARRATIVES OF AFFIRMATIVE ACTION

In the larger societal understandings of African American success is the important narrative that many successful people of color are often undeserving, and they often find themselves engaged in discussions in which they have to defend their accomplishments. Much of this follows the overall societal pattern of racial discussions through the idea of white victimology—the idea that whites, specifically white males, are now victims of a system of racial oppression, largely because of people of color. One such narrative involves the larger belief that African Americans are entering the industry, with lesser qualifications, because of affirmative action or larger race-based policies. In this particular narrative, there is never the consideration that those African Americans hired to be pilots are aptly qualified or that those whites not hired lack the appropriate qualifications.[28] As many whites usually share these narratives in various settings, there has become a collective and broader narrative concerning unfair treatment of whites that spills over into their interactions with African Americans in the industry, specifically when it comes to the position of pilot. This is suggested in the many interactions in which whites openly challenge black authority and pose questions concerning their qualifications.

In interactions with their co-workers, pilots report much animosity by whites resulting from the narrative of affirmative action. In many of these cases, whites do not mask their discomfort with black pilots, but instead openly discuss the general idea of airlines hiring those that are less than fully qualified, all the while insinuating that a qualified white person did not get hired due to "racist practices." During a hearing based on the airline industry, a report was presented to Congress by the Government Activities and Transportation Subcommittee of the House Committee on Government Operations and found that many major airlines failed to "institutionalize and incorporate affirmative action into corporate policy" (Hansen and Oster 1997:118). Be that as it may, the narrative that unqualified African Americans are given positions continues to be a mainstay in the airline industry.

> I was on the jump seat one time on National Airlines trying to get home from Newark and the captain and FO (first officer), they were having a conversation and the FO said something like, "You know I was flying with this guy and you know he was one of those guys I could tell got his job from affirmative action." And I just kind of sat there . . . I'm getting a free ride home, but I could just tell, the captain, like he got uneasy like right away, he kind of just looked back over his shoulder and I had my head down. I was looking like this [demonstrates with his head down]. I could tell he was kind of like . . . his face was saying, "Man, shut up!" and the FO didn't catch it right away; he just kept talking and stuff.

Note that this first officer did not need to provide any concrete evidence for his claim of affirmative action, but he felt free to voice his opinions even in the presence of his black colleague. In this case, the actions of the white actor insinuate his ideology of the inferior nature of people of color by suggesting that the person he recently flew with was a product of affirmative action and not merely a qualified pilot. In this, there is the dismissal of success and a reification of white racial rhetoric. For this white first officer to state, "I could tell [he was one of those guys that] got his job from affirmative action" shows that race, as the significant marker of ability and skill, is thus another example that African Americans in this industry are judged heavily by their "racial uniform."

On another occasion, with pain in his voice, a young male pilot shared a somewhat similar story:

> Well, I was flying with one guy, and it is rare that I agree with the guy that is sitting next to me. Most of the guys I fly with are between the ages of forty-five and sixty, white males, so, we don't agree on a lot and that's understandable. Many of the guys are very professional; we listen to each other's opinions and agree to disagree. But it was one guy that was very condescending and insulting with his opinions. We kinda went back and forth. I thought it was over with when the trip was over. On one of his off days, he went into a store that one of my friends was working at. I have been knowing this girl for many years, so when he told her he was a pilot for the airline, she asked if he knew me . . . He says, "Yeah, I know him." He had the nerve to tell her that he felt

that the only reason I was hired was because of affirmative action, that I was
unqualified to do my job and that there were many other white pilots still at
regional carriers that have been there longer that should have been hired here
ahead of me.

Here, it is important to highlight the connections many whites make to the
skill set of African American pilots. The notion that positions were not
earned remains indicative of how a great many whites *feel* about and *perceive* black pilots. Many of the participants in this project noted the common
assumption held by co-workers that they are unfairly given opportunities to
become pilots. In this is an expression of white anger and backlash at the
growing numbers of women and men of color in the flight deck (though these
numbers remain extremely small!). For many whites, the overestimation of
the numbers of people of color and women in the industry is but one way to
rationalize the narrative that the airline industry is treating whites unfairly.
The encompassing ideology that African Americans are entering the flight
deck with subpar qualifications continues to place these flight crews in the
undue position of defending their abilities. This defense has an emotional
dimension, including feelings of disappointment, anger, and frustration at the
thought that there is not much that can be done to change this frame created
by whites.

RACIAL "OTHERS" AND EMPTY KITCHENS:
WHITE ATTEMPTS AT MALE BONDING

In the many narratives that take place behind the confined walls of the flight
deck, there are also conversations of the racialized "other" and of women. In
many ways, this can be seen as an attempt to bond with these African
American pilots as though there is a common and shared perception of other
racial ethnic groups and of women. Though these opinions are usually openly
discussed, many African American pilots noted their discomfort with these
conversations, yet they were conducted in a way to discourage counternarratives. The frequency in which African American pilots mentioned these conversations is staggering. For instance, one pilot noted:

> In the cockpit, there is also talk of other races. They love to make comments
> about Mexicans and immigration and all of that and it's the same thing. I try
> not to engage in it, and if it gets too out of hand then I will say something
> against it. When they get too aggressive with it, I just say, "This was Mexico
> anyway. This was their land. Just get used to it." When you are sitting there
> and all of your duties are done, race comes up a lot.

Discussions of various racial and ethnic groups and also discussions of
women often take place behind the closed door of the flight deck. In many

ways, these attempts to engage in these various dialogues can be seen as a method of male bonding over common assumptions about "other" people of color and white women, but they serve to widen the gap between these pilots. These black pilots take these conversations to heart with a stealth awareness of "If I weren't here, what would the conversation be about?" In another example, a young male pilot noted,

> It's generally in the context of somebody readin' the paper and some story is on there about, let's say for instance, this Arizona stuff that's goin' on. Somebody will make a comment like, "Yeah, we do need to secure the border from these people," you know, that kind of talk. When I hear stuff like that, you just listen to them and just look at them and just ignore them. If it's not someone that's not a total idiot you can say something with an opposing view and they get the hint there. So they can be talking about women or other people and I have said, "Well, men do that, too." And then they look at me as to say, "I almost forgot—*you're not one of us.*"

For many of these pilots, discussions of other racial and/or ethnic groups serves as a reminder that these racialized discussions are not limited to interactions between them and their white colleagues. It places them in the position of "imagining" what conversations are about when they are not in the flight deck or when there are only white pilots having these discussions. Because these conversations are open discussions, they have an awareness that there is a high likelihood that negative commentaries concerning members of their racial group may very well be the topic of conversation when they are not around. It is very likely they are correct; much racist dialogue on African Americans is discussed outside of their presence—in those hidden backstage (and frontstage, as we have seen) places. Important, too, in these examples is the implication of the racialized experiences of all people of color in this industry. Indeed, the implicit assumption that these African American males would willingly engage in these conversations—to temporarily be considered *almost* one of the guys—serves as a reminder that they are not a part of the culture, as noted by the pilot in his awareness of "you're not one of us."

Take, for instance, another account of this "bonding conversation" started by a white captain:

> Well, in the cockpit there is often talk about women. We have a common frequency that we use on the radio for transactions. I remember this time that a woman came on the frequency and the man next to me said, "Another empty kitchen." But the thing is, I'm thinking, why would you say that? So, when you are flying with another white guy and you hear my voice do you say, "Another empty jail cell?" I mean, why would you say that? That doesn't even go through my mind when I hear a woman's voice on the radio . . . it is never any thought that she shouldn't be there.

The reference to an empty kitchen in reference to women purports the idea that the position of pilot is one that is reserved for males. The steepness of this general sexist ideology of women, as belonging in the household, perpetuates the existing hierarchy of racial and gendered "others" as belonging anywhere but the flight deck. Noting the reaction of the black pilot as one in which he contemplates the possible white, stereotypical thoughts of African American males, requires emotional labor to be performed in reference to resisting sexist ideologies while also providing deep analysis of his position on the aircraft. Though different in many ways from the experiences of women, there is a collective understanding that the comments of the captain serve as an exclusionary mechanism against women and people of color.

As a blatant method of calling attention to the white women and African Americans working for the company, one pilot discussed the ways white pilots differentiated women and African Americans in the following way:

> We are a smaller airline and people hire their friends and they protect their friends, and you can get away with a lot of things because the higher ups are friends. So there is a bunch of insensitivity there. They thought it was funny and they thought they could get away with things. So they titled people to say that I am better than you, like, "I'm flying with C2." "Oh, I flew with her a few weeks ago and she didn't give up anything." . . . So, they also named the few black pilots that were there at the time N1, N2, and N3 to signify Nigger 1, Nigger 2, and Nigger 3. For women, that C1, C2, and C3 was for Cunt 1, Cunt 2, and Cunt 3.

In this example, this pilot shares an (un)official method many pilots used to talk about the few women and African Americans who were employed at his airline. This overtly racist and sexist language is indicative of a larger understanding of how some white males engaged in discussions that would cement not only their perceived superior status but also to allow those women and African Americans to be aware of their perceived inferior status. Collectively, many of these conversations that take place in the workplace, whether about racial and ethnic groups or women, are simply mechanisms to claim the space as well as the position of pilot as one that they cannot enter. The harsh reality of knowing you are labeled "C1" or "N1" instead of by your name is an emotional burden placed on the backs of white women and people of color by white peers and implicitly by those in management. Because this pilot mentions the fact that the airline is small and the majority of those in management are "friends," the deception of the "old-boy network" at its core is an *old-white-boy* network. This everyday sanctioning of underrepresented groups is taken for granted by many whites in the industry, yet it is deeply connected to the complexity of working in an industry where emotional labor, as an aspect of job performance, is suddenly constant.

As discussed in the previous sections, the rhetoric of affirmative action, of racialized others, and of women reveals important aspects to consider as we move into a more inclusive discussion of emotional labor (chapter 4). In this racialized and gendered occupation of airline pilot, African Americans and other racial groups are indeed not the only groups that face discriminatory actions. As white women and women of color continue to move into this industry, they, too, pose a concern for white males that consider the space to be for white males only.

GOLF, GUNS, AND MUSIC:
GENDER, RACE, AND CLASS ON THE FLIGHT DECK

In the existing social science literature on emotional labor, gender has been a long-standing lens through which to understand emotional labor, management, and performance. Even in this, those women in the airline industry, specifically pilots, are faced with the added dimension of being in a position in which they are significantly underrepresented. Over the years, women have made significant efforts to gain entry into this industry through various legal means. Still, there is the remaining larger ideology that they do not belong in the flight deck. Intersecting experiences of race and gender must be placed in context in order to fully understand emotional labor. Much like the dimension of race and the historical and systemic foundation of racial oppression in our country, sexism, too, has deep, oppressive roots that should be taken into account when examining the experiences of flight crews. Instances involving gender, much like race, should not be separated from the theoretical propositions and foundations of emotional labor.

As noted earlier, women are often the subject of numerous conversations that take place in the flight deck. As most all of the pilots interviewed for this project mentioned, the various stereotypical views of women were done in a way that these pilots were able to connect to the similarities in language surrounding them. Much like the opening comment above, the intersecting nature of race and gender is evoked in such a way that cannot be separated. For instance, in my discussion with a black female pilot, she noted:

> The weird thing is that passengers always think I'm a flight attendant. I show up in uniform and the gate agents even think I'm a flight attendant. In my uniform, with my hat and everything, they still assume I'm a flight attendant. For them, it just doesn't make sense. They are programmed to see pilots as gray-haired guys and here I am and they are like, I don't see your name here. I have to point it out to them. When I'm not in the cockpit, passengers think I'm a flight attendant also.

As will be discussed in more detail in the next chapter, there is an assumption that the occupation of flight attendant is gendered, as seen in the above account of the female pilot. Interestingly, she notes that it is not only passengers making the assumption of her position on the aircraft but also those who work in this environment on a regular basis. To examine the job of flight attendant as being gendered misses the idea here that much of this assumption about her position also has much to do with her racial identity as well as her gender; it is in the idea that she does not belong in the flight deck. Adam, a young male pilot, noted having similar experiences:

> With co-workers, I often wonder if my race is a factor. I have talked to other black pilots about this to see if they have had similar experiences and they have. There is always separate paperwork; there is paperwork for the flight attendants, and paperwork that is to be given to the pilots. Now, for those that work for the company, pilot and flight attendant uniforms look nothing alike. But in some places, they will give me the flight attendant paperwork. There is nothing I can do with that. I have never seen flight attendants given pilot paperwork. The only pilots I have heard of getting flight attendant paperwork has been blacks and women. I have gotten on the airplane in full pilot uniform: hat, tie, flight bags. Then the caterer will ask me if I am working first class. But it is something to be mistaken for a flight attendant by your own co-workers who do this every day. This happens to blacks and to female pilots.

Jordan noted similar experiences:

> I've seen that where uh . . . I'm flying with a female captain and they automatically think I'm the captain or think she's a flight attendant. Or the other thing that happens is they think I'm security! Before TSA changed their shirts to blue they used to be white. I was always mistaken as security, so I mean that was a big thing, like when I was in LA, "Yeah, all right, the bathroom's right there" (laughter). You know what I mean?

These cases of "mistaken identity" go far beyond being innocent mistakes but are suggestive of greater ideologies concerning the appropriate positions of women and people of color manifested through these miscues. Long-standing notions that women are relegated to more caring and service roles are also connected to the ideas of these individuals being racialized and gendered in such a way to reduce their positions to those of invisibility. The view that women, in many respects regardless of race, and men of color do not belong in the flight deck continues to show the interconnectivity between racialized and gendered industries, larger society, and those systemic perspectives of women and people of color in general. This shows, too, that within spaces that are disproportionately male and overwhelmingly white, those not fitting this description are ideologically placed in inferior positions.

With this, a racialization of people as well as particular locales occurs, as in the above example of a pilot "always mistaken as security."

In a similar vein, several of the black male pilots noted other ways in which gender identity contributed to their interactions in the flight deck. As mentioned earlier in this chapter, black males, even when they fly as captain, often deal with those who work for the company entering the flight deck and automatically speaking with their white colleague, and there are those occasions in which a different pattern emerges. For instance, a few pilots noted an interesting story:

> Well, I am sure I would notice it more if I was a woman, but I have seen how this industry treats women. I try to be protective because of that. It's not nice. I've seen the jokes that males make about women, and every female that I have flown with has been excellent, just a joy to be around. Now and then people will come up front and there are certain things that you have to get approved from the captain—you can't just ask either pilot. They've asked me and I am quick to say, "That's the captain." I try to correct them as quickly as possible. But, I think black women have it the worst. There are just so few of them. I mean there are more white females than blacks, period.

Another pilot working for an altogether different airline noted a similar experience he has had when flying with female captains:

> I have been flying with a female captain before and what I have seen people do is—and it's disrespectful—they will—in general when something is wrong with the plane—they will just go to the captain [like maintenance, for instance]. Well, they come up and they see the two of us sitting there and there is a female sitting there, they will immediately turn to the male FO and start talking and totally ignore the captain. That would never happen under any other circumstance . . . its only because it's a female that they would do something so disrespectful. It's happened when I've been sitting there and I am like, yes, I am up here, but she is the one that is responsible. We have the joke that three stripes stand for "not my responsibility."

In the above examples, the significance of gender identity in the flight deck is apparent through the invisibility experienced by female pilots regardless of racial identity. Though a majority of the pilots interviewed in this project did not note this occurrence, several provided insight into the intricacies of the role of gender. As we saw earlier, black captains often experience these slights to their position when flying with a white male first officer, but when flying with female captains, though race was not mentioned, they are often excluded from the position of captain. There is a larger connection of sexism at play in the experiences of these women in the gendered framing of women and the appropriate positions they are to occupy. In these cases, those working for the company reify the masculine nature of flying, even when taking into account racial identity. In these instances, the flight deck is not only a context with the normative structure of whiteness, as in the case of black pilots, but there is also the normative ideology that it is also structurally a male space. What should be noted in these accounts is the frequency in which black male pilots spoke up on behalf of their white female colleagues—a benefit not afforded them by their white male copilots. Building on the idea that the occupation of pilot is seen as a male space, Tina noted her experience when she decided to have a baby:

> I was pregnant for the first time . . . I was the first black female there and something as simple as getting a uniform, they had no idea what to do with me. They were all, "I'm not sure where you would go." That was kind of weird to me, you know. I have to have a uniform, but they didn't have anything in place. I was commuting, and I went and asked for the jump seat, and I am in the jet way waiting and this guy from my airline comes down the jet way and he makes this comment. He said, "You need to read what it says in the ops [operations] manual about uniform attire." At first I was smiling but then my face changed. So, as I get on the airplane, it hit me what he said. He didn't even know that I was wearing a maternity uniform. He sits up here and thinks that I'm being sloppy with my shirt out . . . Well, when I get on the plane, I go over to him and say, "I'm pregnant and this is the maternity uniform." He just looks at me. He doesn't apologize or nothing.

In this account, there are larger connections between the ideology of women, the role of those higher up in the organization, and gendered interactions. As noted here, there is a mention that those in the company did not know "what to do with me." There were no particular measures in place to adequately deal with pregnancy, thereby implying that this is indeed a male industry. Even though women entered this industry in the 1970s, the fact that a maternity uniform posed a problem notes that, though regulations changed, the input and needs of women were not fully included. In this interaction, the co-worker sanctioned the female pilot for being "sloppy" and not fully understanding what the policy states about uniform attire. In this, there is the inherent privilege of masculinity through his direct confrontation of her uniform and the notion that he did not have to take the time to recognize her uniform as a maternity uniform fitting well within the guidelines provided by the company. This privilege also allowed the acting pilot the larger idea that it is appropriate to "call out" the female pilot without taking the time to have a conversation with her. In the end, no apology was given, indicating that her mere presence was wrong, not his ideology. Many of the male pilots interviewed for this project noted the frequency in which women are discussed in a sexist manner behind the closed door; it is apparent that women are still considered outsiders that happened to slip into one of the front seats. Indeed, all of the women in this project, much like the men, discussed the frequency of the interactions in which they are "reinterviewed" and told, "I don't think you are ready to fly this aircraft . . . I would like to see you in something smaller." This shines light on the role of sexism on the aircraft. Here, too, all noted they felt "scrutinized" because of their gender, and there were those cases in which they were ignored, much like their black male counterparts:

> I'd say being a woman, you are more scrutinized from day one. When I was twenty-one, I worked at a hotel near JFK and I would talk to the corporate pilots a lot and tell them that I was learning how to fly, and some of them would just make nasty comments like, "Well, you're too old." They'd talk to me like I'm a piece of dirt, you know . . . When I was a commuter pilot there was actually one guy that refused to talk to me because he thought I was going to get on with a major airline before him because of my sex and race. He just despised me. It's amazing.

Connected to the larger narratives created insisting that African Americans are receiving unfair advantages in the industry is also the connection with the important example of exclusion. These narratives, along with many others, are done in a way that rationalizes large-scale exclusion and scrutiny. The airline industry, as it has been historically grounded in larger U.S. society with specific hierarchies of race and gender, still maintains those remnants through contemporary methods of sexism and gender discrimination. Collectively, gender and racial identity offer a unique experience for these pilots, one that should be included in our social science understandings of emotion work and emotional labor. These interlocking systems of oppression facilitate a working environment with gendered and racialized experiences similar to those experienced outside of work. For many of these individuals, the ability to escape gendered and racialized experiences becomes quite difficult, and there is an inability to be protected from experiences based on race and gender in the workplace; indeed, the work environment proves to be a large part of the problem.

There are also those subtle representations of race and gender that creep into the interactions between these pilots. Although many pilots discussed blatant discriminatory behavior during training, there were also those instances in which "cultural differences" were important. Tina notes:

> Yes, there have been those times. But I guess I try to learn something from it. I noticed that when we are in training they would put these metaphors or jokes in the PowerPoints that deal with golf and everyone else was getting it, but I didn't get it. So I had to learn about golf. I don't know what you would call that. Would that be cultural differences? I said, "Well, this is the environment I'm in, let me go learn about this so that I can better relate." In the end, I know a lot about airplanes and that is important.

Here, this pilot notes the use of metaphors during training that she did not understand and often found herself having to go and learn more about golf so that she could better relate to her co-workers as well as understand the relationships between golf and flying airplanes. Though subtle, there are implications of class and gender and, as she believes, "culture." This is not to say that African Americans do not play golf, but it is to say that in an area such as training, metaphors pertaining to the job should be something that all can relate to. There is the incorrect assumption that all those present would be aware of golf analogies. Another pilot mentioned similar experiences with his co-workers:

> There were a lot of times I just couldn't relate to some of my co-workers. People that are from the same background, you know, they have a lot in common already, you know, just kind of a good ole boys club that I didn't get in. Like they would discuss music and people would talk about their favorite bands, I just never heard of these people. I mean, they are talking to each other like, "Aw, man, don't you just love Ted Nugent [laughs]," and they would just say all these names of bands and play the music and I would just be like—I have no idea. They'd talk about hunting and their favorite deer stand and what kind of gun they use and I don't know. I can't really relate.

For these black pilots, there is a level of exclusion and disconnection that they feel based on the conversations that take place in training and on the flight deck. There are those larger connections between gender, race, and class in many respects that serve as dividers between these pilots and their co-workers. The subtle method of exclusion, in this example, implicit in their love of Ted Nugent, a figure known for racist and sexist outbursts, reminds the black pilot of an existing network from which he is excluded.[29]

CONCLUSION

In this chapter, I introduced the idea that systemic racism, as a theoretical foundation of emotions, emotional management, and emotional labor, should also be included as a backdrop to understanding interactions in the workplace. African Americans in the airline industry find themselves facing an industry that was developed during a period in U.S. history in which the racial and gendered framing of women and people of color relegated them to inferior positions. In this, there has been a systematic exclusion in the airline industry, and it has been only recently that African Americans and white women were allowed to enter the industry. Though contemporary methods of exclusion have changed in a number of ways, these ideas must be situated within the larger context in which contemporary notions of racism and sexism have developed because of their systemic nature.

Many existing theories on emotional labor examine the current interactions in the workplace without directly connecting industries to their formation in a system that largely excluded certain peoples from participation. Emotional labor, the weight it carries, and how it is performed can be better understood by connecting it to the larger systems in which it operates. As a representation of how society once functioned to exclude individuals, the airline industry serves as but one location documenting the normative structures once representative of larger society. This industry, and the position of pilot, has expectations of emotional labor that would likely be missed if experiences based on racial and gendered identity were excluded. Emotional labor and emotion work in those interactions based on race and gender are performed *in addition to* the emotional labor that is required to be performed as an aspect of the job. There are those expected areas, such as passenger and safety concerns, that call for the performance of emotional labor, yet what should be included in this is the way in which emotional labor must also be performed when based on those salient racial and gender features that cannot be changed to induce appropriate feeling in others.

The occupation of pilot has been racialized and gendered in a way that reinforces normative expectations of whiteness and maleness. In this, there are also expectations concerning appropriate emotions, methods of interaction, and subsequent emotional labor that are performed by these people of color in what is considered a white institutional space. This poses an altogether different set of expectations and boundaries; maneuvering through notions of superiority and privilege that they are not granted has implications for all involved. For the African Americans interviewed here, emotional labor is not simply relegated to the work required once the boarding door has closed; it is a double shift that actually starts as soon as they are in uniform. The simple acts of leaving the hotel, walking through the terminal, and getting through the gate agents are proven to be not simple, but provide a multitude of areas in which emotional labor is performed. As representatives of their companies, there are standards in place for customer and co-worker interactions that are an aspect of the job. Specifically, when working in an industry and occupation in which there are stereotyped notions of what a pilot "is" and "does" that these individuals do not "fit," there are those intricate details of emotional labor that should be understood within the context of the industry, the society in which it was created, and the role identity plays in the performance of emotional labor. Continuing with this, in the next chapter I examine the role of gender, race, and class with a deeper look at the experiences of African American flight attendants.

Chapter Three

On Display at All Times: Flight Attendants

I have to tell you something that happened to my friend recently; it didn't happen to me, but I had one of my girl friends share this with me . . . She's on the 757 standing at the door and this little [white] boy comes on . . . He looks at my friend who is African American and says, "Are you a monkey?" She was like, "Excuse me?" He's like, "Are you a monkey?" And his mom is like, "Todd!!" and he's still like, "Are you a monkey" and she's like, "No, baby, I'm not a monkey," and she said to their credit there were some white people sitting around and they seemed embarrassed.[1]

Imagine for a moment that you are the flight attendant in this story. As you perform your job, you are asked publicly if you are a monkey. This race-laden, centuries-old depiction of African Americans as monkeys is hurtful, demoralizing, and dehumanizing, and it happens in a context in which the flight attendant is constrained in her options of responses. This flight attendant received no support from others (except embarrassment from a few white passengers), nor did the parent of this child require her child to offer an apology. The emotional labor performed by the flight attendant in this case can only be imagined as she states, "No, baby, I'm not a monkey." This very recent connection between African Americans and animals, specifically when referenced by a child, is merely one reminder that our racist history is still unwilling to die. For instance, there have been many cases in which President Obama and his family, including his children, have been depicted as monkeys through various media outlets.[2]

In the previous chapter on African American pilots, I focused on the connections to systemic racism and sexism to lead into a discussion of the deeper connections between social identity and emotional labor. In this chapter, I examine the similarities and differences experienced by flight crews to show that there are several factors that should be in the forefront when discussing how emotional labor is performed in environments that are structurally and culturally white spaces. Since the work of Hochschild, published in the 1980s, there have been many demographic shifts in those working in the job of flight attendant. Not only has the workforce gotten older generally but it has also gotten more diverse in terms of the number of racial-ethnic group members and white males entering the industry.[3] Much earlier, this occupation allowed the flight attendant "the upper-class freedom to travel and participate in the glamour" attached with the notion of flying.[4] Since the 1980s, the industry has changed to one that provides easier access to those passengers who, in the past, might not have had the opportunity to fly due to cost. In many ways, changes in the nature of the industry have removed a great deal of the glamour earlier attached to the job of flight attendant. In turn, demographic shifts have occurred not only for workers but also passengers. Even with these changes, there remain specific expectations of the flight attendant in terms of passenger interactions and company standards. In this chapter, I examine interactions with passengers as well as those interactions with co-workers. As argued in earlier chapters, the connections between emotional labor and service workers should be inclusive of the emotional labor performed outside of those interactions with passengers. Much like pilots, flight attendants spend considerable time in the company of other flight attendants, pilots, and other company personnel. This creates many interactions in which the intersection of race, gender, and class play a major role. The environment of the aircraft is also significant in this analysis because though there have been many demographic shifts, the expectations of flight attendants are in many ways contradictory to the white expectations of people of color.

As I continue to examine the micro interactions flight attendants deal with, I combine this with the larger macro processes that directly influence these interactions. Thus, although much has changed to reflect changes in gender and race ideologies, even more remains the same. The long-standing stereotypical notions concerning gender, class, and race are continuously reflected in the interactions of these flight attendants. Much like the pilots I discussed in an earlier chapter, flight attendants also contend with racialized and gendered interactions that contribute largely to their performance of emotional labor. For flight attendants, "the smiles are a *part of her work*, a part that requires her to coordinate self and feeling so that the work seems effortless. Similarly, part of the job is to disguise fatigue and irritation, for otherwise the labor would show in an unseemly way, and the product—passenger contentment—would be damaged" (Hochschild 1983:8, emphasis in original). Here, it is important to provide inquiry into what it means for workers and passengers when many of the interactions are heavily influenced by preconceived ideologies and framing based on race, gender, and class, all within the context of corporate expectations of professionalism. Flight attendants, unlike pilots, spend a majority of their workday interacting with passengers and are seen as those representing the airline as frontline employees. But much like those pilots, fight attendants have a limited escape from adverse interactions. They are literally trapped in a confined space from which they cannot escape for hours at a time, no matter how difficult their interactions with passengers and co-workers may be. In these multiple interactions, there is a deeper connection between emotion work and racialized and gendered stereotypes. These connections between identity and interactions are but one aspect of a bigger, broader stratified system that contribute to how emotional labor is performed in the workplace.

Much like the pilots I discussed earlier, flight attendants experience multiple types of exclusion. As described by these flight attendants, there is an invisibility to their positions on the aircraft and an insensitivity undergirding their relationships with passengers and co-workers. In performing this job, there were particular expectations concerning passengers that were seen as a large part of being a flight attendant. Luggage concerns, weather delays (and turbulence), along with passenger expectations with beverages and/or food are significant areas of work where emotional labor is needed, but there are also those experiences that are discussed in more private circles, among friends and family—those interactions based on the unchangeable features of race and gender that also contribute greatly to everyday emotion work.

While many of their experiences are similar to those mentioned in the work of Hochschild, there are also distinct differences. One such difference occurs when passenger interactions with flight attendants are based on the collectivity of their gender and racial identity. In addition, flight attendants spend much time considering how to counter these interactions in the course of their workday. Here, I connect the contextual significance of the environment (the aircraft), systemic racism and sexism, and the relationship of the "actor" to flight attendants in order to argue that emotion work and emotional labor should not be disconnected from the structural systems creating, constricting, and contributing to how emotional labor is performed.

COLORED "GIRLS," GERM CARRIERS, AND SEX OBJECTS: BLACK FLIGHT ATTENDANTS ON DISPLAY

In Hochschild's work on emotional labor and flight attendants, an examination of the gendered interactions that take place between flight attendants and passengers was understood from the perspective of the flight attendant and the expectations of management in terms of customer service and professionalism. In this idea, flight attendants were expected to wear smiles and learn effective ways to handle irate passengers. During those years in which

Hochschild conducted research, there were indeed expectations of what was representative of flight attendants that contributed to the overall nature of the industry. Airline advertising insinuating the nature of those women in the industry often enhanced sexualized ideologies of flight attendants. For instance, Hochschild notes that advertising during this time had sexual overtones. Continental Airlines ran an ad: "We really move our tails for you to make your every wish come true . . . "National ran the ad": Fly me, you'll like it."[5] These ads, coupled with the fact that most flight attendants during this time were young women, led to an image of the sexualized flight attendant and reified their subordinate position to men. For instance, Eastern Airlines would give men little black books to "collect stewardesses' phone numbers."[6] Outside of the "created" sexualized image of flight attendants, there was also the racialized image of the flight attendant as white.

Regarding the process airlines used to select applicants, attributes such as friendliness and a warm personality were often used by airlines, but when discussing what this meant to the flight attendants, "[o]ne United worker explained: 'United wants to appeal to Ma and Pa Kettle. So it wants Caucasian girls—not so beautiful that Ma feels fat, and not so plain that Pa feels unsatisfied. It's the Ma and Pa Kettle market that's growing, so that's why they use the girl-next-door image to appeal to that market.'"[7] Here, the "girl-next-door" ideology is directly connected to a particular race, gender, and class identity. In this notion of the girl-next-door, where do African Americans fit, and how did the systematic exclusion of African Americans contribute to the development of an industry in which whites (women) were seen as the "ideal type"? Much like African American pilots, African American flight attendants only gained entry into the industry through a series of court cases, and the first African American flight attendant was hired in 1958. In an industry set up and advertised as white, there were not many direct connections to African American women in the industry. Because of this, there was a long-standing notion of what a flight attendant should be and how they should perform.

At the time African Americans entered the industry as flight attendants, the civil rights movement was introducing many new opportunities, but the racial framing of African Americans as inferior was deeply embedded in the minds of many white Americans. In this negative racial framing were also specific ideologies of gender that led to forms of gendered racism against women and men of color. These structural creations of gendered and racialized beliefs transitioned into the workforce, contributing to emotional labor. At this juncture, it is important to insist that although much mainstream understandings of race and gender suggest we have achieved equality, the experiences of people of color in the workplace show this "improvement" to be superficial. For instance, in an interview with Cindy, a senior African

American female flight attendant, she discussed a recent encounter on the aircraft with a passenger as follows:

> The one that stands out for me was I was working first class and there's a lady in the back that was having some problems with the flight attendants in the back. It was three white flight attendants back there, and I was the *only black woman* on the plane. She gets upset with them for whatever, so they come and tell me about this lady in the exit row in the back. Well, the woman says, "I don't want to speak to any of y'all; I want to speak to the colored girl." I didn't hear this, but one of them came up front and says, "There is a woman who is really upset back there and she wants to talk to you only. She only wants to talk to the colored girl." I said, "Oh, really? Colored girl, huh? Well, tell her the *colored girl* will be back there in just a minute."

In this account, the white female passenger made direct connections to gender and racial identity. As this passenger states, she wanted to speak with the "colored girl"; she assumed a position of superiority, power, and domination by calling on a distinct and painful past in which African Americans were referenced as "colored" and as "girl or boy." This implies that she is not seen as a woman but is placed in a subordinate position by this passenger (and many of those hearing this characterization). This distorted language also references a much more dominant ideology that is a characterization of the larger society. As a black woman, this flight attendant must not only contend with those things connected to being a flight attendant (irate passengers) but must also handle the expectations held of her as a woman of color. In this particular account, there are larger implications for interactions that are based on what it means to be a "colored" flight attendant.

Here, too, it is important to note the actions of her co-workers. Not only did they relay this racist language, but Cindy, the flight attendant affected, noted that they "snickered" when telling her that a passenger in the back wanted to speak with the colored girl. In this case, they did not correct the passenger on her flawed reference to their co-worker but left the flight attendant to deal with the passenger who insulted her as well as with the consequence of correcting her. In these types of encounters, the direct connections to gender and race, along with the systemic connections to U.S. history, are indeed outside of the scope of much of the work on emotional labor. Here, the interconnectivity between systemic racism and sexism and emotional labor shows how they cannot be dissected and reduced to an either-or scenario, but that the consequence of systemic racism/sexism is one fundamental dimension of performing emotional labor. Additionally, the awareness of this flight attendant that she was the *only* African American on the entire aircraft is of extreme significance and is indicative of her alienation. To relieve pressure, vent, or engage in a discussion with someone about this hurtful and offensive act is limited, as she is "racially alone," flying with those that find humor in her being called a "colored girl." Cindy's co-workers and other passengers reiterated her racialization by relaying the message and through their abandonment of Cindy. Indeed, this emotionally laborious process was not shared but was hers alone.

As flight attendants are seen as providing the greatest amount of customer service to passengers, there are those inherent connections to the idea that this is what women *are supposed to do*. In many cases, both those women interviewed in this project as well as those in Hochschild's work connect larger ideas of sexism and images of women. In an interview Hochschild conducted with a flight attendant, the flight attendant notes,

> Now, if a man calls out to me, "Oh, waitress," I don't like it. I'm not a waitress. I'm a flight attendant. But I know that sometimes they just don't know what to call you, and so I don't mind. But if they call me "honey" or "sweetheart" or "little lady" in a certain tone of voice, I feel demeaned, like they don't know that in an emergency I could save their chauvinistic lives. (1983:28)

Using this example provided by Hochschild, it is clear that in this case, there are also direct connections between gender and the historical context of how women were viewed by larger society. Those males in these cases that use the language of "little lady" suggest that women are viewed from a subordinate position and are treated as such. As this flight attendant makes a direct connection to sexism, there are also differences seen from the flight attendants in Hochschild's work and those interviewed for this project. Again, when factoring in racial identity, African American flight attendants experienced an altogether different racialized language and broader framing directly connected to their gender. "Little lady" and "colored girl," though both derogatory and sexist, also carry vastly different historical meanings.

Many of the flight attendants in this project noted connections between race, gender, and the much larger assumptions of servitude that are often influenced greatly by these intersecting identities. Granted, many flight attendants, even those included in Hochschild's earlier work, noted their distaste of the term *waitress*. But these black flight attendants extended those views of white flight attendants as waitress and connected them with much broader themes of an African American flight attendant as *servant*. Though passengers often use the terminology of *waitress* to black flight attendants, *waitress* to them is done in such a way that it carries the implicit meaning of *servant*:

> As black flight attendants . . . some of them look at you as a real servant. But it goes beyond this. People have a sense of entitlement. It's usually white women between the ages of twenty-five and sixty. Every last one of them! Especially from us; we're supposed to do every last thing they ask us to. It's like I'm a personal servant or something. I call it the jump, snap, and roll. I had a young

white girl throw her bag down and tell me to stow it. I'm looking at her and thinking, I'm twice her age. How you gone talk to me like that . . . The older business women do it maybe because they are used to telling their employees to do this [respondent is snapping her fingers and pointing]. So they get on the plane and look at us and we at that same level as the person that runs and gets their coffee, according to them. They can tell us when to hop, skip, and jump . . . They expect us to be the mother, the nanny, the maid, and the doctor. All of that.

Here, this flight attendant recognizes the expectations of her that are outside of the scope of what constitutes being a flight attendant. As she notes that she believes she is seen as a real servant, she also attaches this to the actions of others. In one case, a young woman insists that the flight attendant stow her bags as though this is how it is supposed to be. This flight attendant did not fully know if she gets ordered to stow luggage because she is perceived to be a servant or because she is seen as *strong*. Perhaps both explanations are likely, and both are racialized. There are connections to class through the mention that many of these encounters are based on a sense of entitlement and the idea that black flight attendants are seen on the same level as the person who "runs and gets their coffee," placing them in the position of "the help." These long-standing racial and gendered ideologies are a part of a deeper structure that subordinates women of color to those roles of servitude. There are also those historical connections to the perceived physical strength of African American women.[8]

Indeed, there were those cases in which African American female flight attendants were demanded to stow the luggage of men. One flight attendant openly discussed a case in which on an aircraft with two aisles (a 767), a white male passenger wanted to pass "his large roller-board to me over the heads of other people from the other aisle. He said, 'Put this in the overhead bins for me.' Here, much like the examples above, there is a historical reality in the relationships between these whites and African American women. As those old stereotypes of race and gender place black women in a seemingly inferior position to white women (though the latter are inferior to white men), much of this is seen in this contemporary example. As Patricia Hill Collins notes in her research on African American women: "Within U.S. culture, racist and sexist ideologies permeate the social structure in such a degree that they become hegemonic, namely seen as natural, normal, and inevitable. In this context, certain assumed qualities that are attached to Black women are used to justify oppression" (2000:5). Note, too, those deeper connections with age in the mention that even young women (or even, young children as seen in the opening account) continue to see black women in a particular role or position. As Feagin (2010) has noted about the white racial frame, much of these overarching ideologies of African Americans are continuously passed through generations through various networks. Another flight attendant, Monica, provides a similar example.

> They see us like a waitress—an upscale waitress, [laughs] or a servant. Because they think we're suppose to do everything; giving me their booger tissues. [laughter] Well, trying to give me, you know, tissue. You know, bodily fluids, clean up my vomit . . . Sometimes snapping at you, you know, snapping a hand. Just like you're, you know, somewhere on the field back in the day. And *that 's* the part of the job I can't handle!

Much like the earlier account, this female flight attendant also notes those larger connections to servitude and associates this with being "somewhere on the field back in the day." Again, this flight attendant extends the idea of being a waitress and includes a more historical understanding of what being an African American in this environment sometimes can mean. These experiences were not limited to female flight attendants; those African American male flight attendants in this project also noted having experiences in which there is a historical significance to their current interactions with passengers. For instance, one male flight attendant (John) recalled an experience with a white male passenger as the passenger loudly stated, "Boy, can you get me some more coffee?" John replied, "Boy? Ain't no boys on here, I'm over thirty." Here, too, the intersection of race and gender is apparent with this passenger referencing him as "boy." In this, there was a direct connection with notions of subservience—understanding that the term *boy* removed not only a level of masculinity but was also reminiscent of a Jim Crow past in which African Americans were openly called *boy* and there was nothing they could do about it. In many of these cases of attempted subordination, there is also the flip side—the elevation of whites. In many of these cases, the racialized and gendered language was blatant, as in the example of the "colored girl" and the references made to the male flight attendant as "boy." However, there are also those deeper understandings provided by these African American flight attendants. The understanding that, though it is believed by mainstream society that the past is the past and there is a larger societal separation of the past and present, these African Americans "recognize how historically rooted present-day racism and gendered racism both are."[9]

These interactions call for much emotional labor to be performed. Recalling the ideology that flight attendants are expected to remain friendly and professional in spite of irate passengers misses the significance of these racialized experiences. Also significant is the frequency in which these encounters occur. Truly, it cannot (and should not) be assumed that African American participants only have these encounters while on the aircraft, but we should recognize that these racial encounters are one more example of the racially patterned interactions taking place in larger society. These accounts on the aircraft are but one location in which these crew members face attacks as women and men of color.

In her discussion of emotional labor and the workforce, Hochschild states,

> But in the public world of work, it is often part of an individual's job to accept uneven exchanges, to be treated with disrespect or anger by a client, all the while closeting into fantasy the anger one would like to respond with. The customer is king, unequal exchanges are normal, and from the beginning customer and client assume different rights to feeling and display. The ledger is supposedly evened by a wage. (1983:85–86)

There is much truth to this statement with regard to public service work. Management quickly teaches those working in a public industry providing customer service that the customer comes first and is always right. But there is also something to be said about these unequal exchanges; where is the line drawn between consumer rights and the civil rights and people of color who face a level of sexism and racism from the customers they are expected to serve? Too, can consistent racism and sexism be offset by wages? Those working during Hochschild's research and these women and people of color currently in the industry are forced to comply with racial and gendered affronts in such a way that implies that these encounters are a normative aspect of a much larger structural system. Problematic for those doing emotional labor is the larger rule in which the customer assumes the rights to feelings and display. Even outside of "ordinary" emotional labor performed on the job, when race, gender, and class characteristics are involved, much of what is seen as appropriate in the workplace is simply a reproduction of what is appropriate in larger society.

The relationships of these flight attendants to the passengers they serve can be bipolar when examined from the larger context. As many note, they are seen as servants—there to provide all the service needs of passengers— but they are also sometimes seen as not capable of providing a service to passengers. As one example of this, several of the flight attendants in this project noted the frequency with which passengers want them to do the heavy work (as in lifting luggage) but prefer them not to serve their drinks. Consider the following example:

> I have had people refuse to take a drink from me and I know it's because I'm black. Like this one time, I was working with this white guy on the cart and I asked this man if he wanted something to drink and he just said, "No." So I said, I'm done, and I asked if I can make anything to the guy that I was working with and he said, "No, I'm ready to move." Then, the man that I'd just asked if he wanted something to drink said to the white guy on the cart, "Excuse me, I'd like something to drink." Now, he tells the white guy that. I

said, "Oh, really, so you didn't want anything from me." Well, he just ignored
me and continued to talk to the white guy about wanting something to drink.

Though these are more often unspoken encounters, they do not fail to
have a racial meaning to those flight attendants involved. As most would
initially assume, there was the possibility that the passenger refused a drink
because he did not want one at the time. But in this particular account, this
flight attendant directly connects this to her racial identity because this passenger immediately asked for a drink from her white colleague and ignored
her when she noted that he asked her colleague and not her.[10] Unfortunately,
these racialized incidents also occurred at an alarming frequency. Another
flight attendant, as did many others, noted that passengers would decline
allowing them to make their drinks. Reasons here ranged from "I don't want
you to touch my cup" to "I just don't want anything." We also have to
consider the public nature of these denials as they are done in the presence of
others. Important for these flight attendants is that though they notice this
behavior, those around them do not and do not have to. This makes these
flight attendants both hypervisible—their blackness is noticed so the passenger refuses the drink—and invisible because their experiences as black wom-
en and men are not observed or validated. Another flight attendant also notes
the frequency in which passengers do not accept drinks from her. She states,
"The one thing that I do notice is a lot of times when we do a service,
somebody that wanted a drink oftentimes will not take a drink from me, and
they will wait until the other flight attendant, particularly if they're Caucasian, will come by and stop them and take the same drink from them." The
statement "a lot of times" in this case implies that this is something that
happens with regularity and is a racialized pattern experienced by African
American flight attendants. We should also recognize that in these particular
cases, flight attendants are expected to continue service as though nothing
happened and with no immediate escape.

SEXUALIZATION OF FEMALE FLIGHT ATTENDANTS

Mentioned earlier in this chapter is the connection between company advertising and the sexualized nature of the job that soon followed. In this, airlines
placed various restrictions on flight attendants that contributed to this sexual
ideology. Earlier, many employees, as cited from Hochschild's work, noted
that this was largely associated with the image of a young, single, white
woman. Because of this, the airline industry effectively created an image of
the flight attendant who was white, attractive, young, and sexually available.
Even as the industry changed, the image of flight attendant stayed much the
same. As we include African American women in the discussions of what is
expected of them, they often find that they, too, are sexualized, but much of

this sexualization is connected to their racial identity, calling forth those stereotyped ideologies of black sexuality. Interestingly, passengers were not the only actors making those sexual advances. One flight attendant recalled this account:

> Now, the pilots are something else . . . They want to court you on the road. They say stuff about how pretty my skin is and they just try you . . . The famous line is, "I like my coffee black, just like I like my women." I think this is a line that they have passed around to each other. They say this all the time. Or they just say, "I like my coffee black . . . *you got any sugar to go with that?*" They would never marry you . . . They just flirt! They just want to see if they have a chance at it.

Again, women of all racial and ethnic groups can be targets of sexism. "However, black women endure a special kind of racialized sexism. Myths about wanton black women abound in this society . . . African American women have long been sexual targets for these men, particularly those with power."[11] In the above example, these advances were made by a pilot, the person seen as in charge of the aircraft. Here, there are deeper connections between the sexualized natures of flight attendant and racial identity as referenced through the coffee analogy. These pervasive images of black female sexuality are seen in many of the white male/black female interactions on the aircraft. These female flight attendants knew well the stereotypes of flight attendants and mentioned that this is one area that is in need of change. A large consensus of flight attendants expressed the belief that one can enter the "mile-high club" with a flight attendant is offensive, disrespectful, and oppressive. As one flight attendant adamantly states,

> There is some stereotypical stuff with flight attendants that needs to be gotten rid of. We are normal and go home to families. We have personal lives outside of flying. I am told by white men all the time that they want to sleep with a flight attendant. They think we get busy with passengers. They want to try you like it's a fantasy.

Many flight attendants noted a similar sexualization by passengers. Another flight attendant recounted the following:

> The public perception of a flight attendant is a waitress in the sky, and some guys see us as being promiscuous. I had one guy, white guy *again*, who I gave a drink. He rang his call light, I gave him a drink, and then he said, "Here, here's a five dollar tip." Well, I said, "That's quite nice of you, sir." "Well, here, you can sit on my lap." I mean he had the five-dollars in his hand and said, "Here's a tip for you" and I told him, no thank, you and then he says, "Well, okay, you can just sit on my lap."

Moreover, another flight attendant noted,

> One insult recently I had was a guy with paper and a pen; a white guy,
> business guy, in a suit, and he is handing it to me, and I'm putting it in the
> trash and he was like, "No, I want your number." That's an insult to me. You
> don't want my number, dude [laughter]. He just assumed I would give it to
> him . . . Isn't that something? Isn't that something? And, he looked at me like I
> should feel lucky. There was also another guy that did that recently . . . an artsy
> LA guy in the music industry. He was very gutsy. But the truth is it's annoy-
> ing. It's usually those white guys . . . everyone thinks they're entitled to things.
> They really think they're entitled to the whole . . . the aircraft belongs to them.
> Everything. Every and anything. Even you and your stuff.

In all these cases, passengers made advances based on those preconceived
ideas of the actions of female flight attendants, specifically those African
American flight attendants. In the earlier account, the flight attendant made
note that this sexual advance was also connected to money and the larger
idea that money would make her more apt to give in to those unwanted
sexual advances. There is a much higher level of social power and privilege
contributing to this interaction, and many of those stereotypes of black wom-
en are located in this account. As Patricia Hill Collins shows in her research
on the experiences of black women, the controlling images of "jezebel,
whore, or 'hoochie'" is a function of a much larger system that seeks to
rationalize treatment of African American women.[12] In the second account,
the flight attendant in this case connects these actions to a sense of "entitlement" that includes "everything on the flippin plane . . . even you and your
stuff." This sense of entitlement is connected to social power, subordination,
and ownership. This ownership is not only of feelings but also ownership of
black female bodies.

In the above cases, flight attendants experience being seen as servants as
well as being spoken to in racially derogatory language and can simultaneously be denied the ability to provide certain aspects of the service. These
seemingly different desires from those white passengers mentioned in these
accounts are but one part of a larger framing of African American women
and men and those interlocking systems of oppression in larger society.
Within the context of work, there are many ways that being a flight attendant
calls for emotional labor, from handling those everyday scenarios with passengers involving luggage, service, and boarding/deplaning issues, to issues
relating to their gender, race, and perceived class background. Conscious and
unconscious ideologies of passengers enter into these interactions, generating
additional emotional labor requirements. In their interactions with passengers
once on the aircraft, there is also a power dynamic that occurs in give-and-
take interactions that leaves these flight attendants taking much more than
they give. With a sense of entitlement, passengers view all things contained

on the aircraft as up for grabs, including the right to voice inappropriate beliefs and the expectation that no counter will be offered. Those passengers board the aircraft with preconceived notions of what is representative of a flight attendant as well as those preconceived notions about people of color, and they often seek out ways to reify a privileged and superior position. This racialized and gendered privilege is reproduced and maintained through the social audience and their silence. Here, too, it is important to note that dealing with passengers is only one aspect of the job; there is also the aspect of dealing with co-workers in confined spaces.

WHO'S IN CHARGE? THE INVISIBILITY OF BLACK AUTHORITY

Much like the African American pilots in the previous chapter, flight attendants reported to a great extent how those around them usurp their earned authority. One such way this is consistently done is through the lack of respect to those positions they work on the aircraft. Here, it is important to remember the historical setup of the industry as one in which flight attendants were usually female and white. This has created an important aspect of the job in which this is usually reiterated in a number of ways; namely, black invisibility on the aircraft. Like the earlier discussion of pilots, the flight attendants also recognize a hierarchy in the cabin. Though there can be many flight attendants on any given flight, there is one flight attendant designated as the "lead" flight attendant. There is a level of authority given this attendant, and she or he is briefed directly by the captain and agents. Flight attendants recognize that many major decisions, as they pertain to customer interactions, are in the hands of the lead. But as mentioned earlier, the industry itself created another hierarchy—one not recognizing African Americans in any capacity in the industry, let alone leadership positions. This dominant ideology of black subordination, portrayed mainly through advertising and company "standards," effectively transitioned into the more mainstream ideal of black visibility and sense of belonging on the aircraft. In her earlier work, Hochschild picked up this pattern and noted:

> A black female flight attendant, who had been hired in the early 1970s when Delta faced an affirmative action suit, wondered aloud why blacks were not pictured in local Georgia advertising. She concluded, "They want that market, and that market doesn't include blacks. They go along with that." Although Delta's central offices were in Atlanta, which is predominantly black, few blacks worked for Delta in *any* capacity. (1983:93, emphasis added)

Missing largely from advertising as well as from the aircraft, there developed a pattern not only in the minds of passengers but also from co-workers. In this section, I seek to highlight some of the interactions that occur with co-workers on board the aircraft. Passenger failure to recognize those in power is indeed something these flight attendants noted, but in this section I focus on how those with the company, who should recognize and know better, usurp the authority of African American flight attendants.

Though not often verbally spoken, the disregard for African Americans working on the aircraft, specifically as pilots and flight attendants, serves as a reaffirmation of white authority and the idea that blacks remain somewhat isolated and invisible in this environment. In the encounters with co-workers, African American flight crew members note the complexities of dealing with other members of the company and the idea of their invisibility on the air-craft. Take the following example provided by a flight attendant with more than twenty-two years of experience:

> I can be sitting on the airplane with my badge on that says "Flight Service Coordinator," and the gate agent will come in, look at me, and then go to the white girl, give her the paperwork, and then say, "Are you ready?" They make the assumption that I can't be in charge; you're black so you can't be the one in charge. And I'm sure it probably happens to the captains. It happens so many times that I just ignore them when they come on. I look at them because they look dead at me and they see my badge but they don't see *me*. They go right to the white girl. The white girl could be at the back of the plane, or they go to the white guy. In other words, *they go right to the white person* and give them all of the paperwork. It happens so much that I just let them walk all the way back there. It's just terrible.

When asked to discuss these experiences in detail, this flight attendant noted the implications of racial identity as well as the significance of gender in this context. When she steps back to examine these interactions, she no-tices that when white flight attendants are present on the aircraft, the assump-tion is that they are in charge, regardless of their gender. Seen largely as a female space, this idea also shows that it is a white space in which whites are generally assumed to have power and be in charge and African Americans are not. This idea that African Americans are not in charge is one that should be placed in a much broader context. Much like larger society, there is a long-standing belief that whites hold superior positions in many industries, even those that have been racialized and/or gendered spaces. Establishing that the aircraft is a white space for pilots should also be extended to flight attendants. The idea here is that the airplane outside the cockpit is foremost a white and largely female space. Most flight attendants discuss the historical reality that the airline industry remained largely white for decades, with increases in black flight attendants being a fairly recent phenomenon, and use this as a method of understanding this behavior. Nevertheless, these flight attendants involved find this a blatant form of disrespect, especially because it comes from those they work with.

The other night I did a trip where I deadheaded to Bogotá and it was a crew of five flight attendants and one captain. And I was not in uniform, there was only one flight attendant that *was* in uniform and the rest of us weren't, so there really was no identification as to who was who, and the captain got on the plane and introduced himself to the two white women, who were seated behind me, never acknowledging me, or that I could potentially be part of the crew. And I can't lie to you and say that it didn't piss me off, because it did. You know, and I was like, I'm not only a flight attendant but the flight attendant in charge! And he has not acknowledged me.[13]

As this flight attendant mentions that the pilot failed to even recognize that she could potentially be a flight attendant, let alone "the flight attendant in charge," there is something to be said of his recognition of the white females as flight attendants. This position, much like the one of pilot, is racialized and gendered in such a way that suggests that though there are significant and increasing numbers of people of color entering this position, it is still normatively construed and structured as white.

It is important to note the frequency of these interactions as they occur as a standard part of work. On any given day or over the course of a multiday trip, consider the fact that in many cases multiple briefings and boardings can and will occur. Also important to recognize is that much of this happens *before* work and interactions with passengers. This bigger-picture perspective lends to the idea that emotion work should be extended to include those frequent, steady interactions with co-workers that can occur multiple times throughout the course of the day. As mentioned in an earlier account by a flight attendant, the assumption that the "white person is in charge" paints a picture of a hierarchy that crosses gender boundaries within the context of the airline industry. Though flight attending is assumed to be a feminine occupation and one largely associated with white women, white males supplant *all* African Americans on the aircraft. One African American male flight attendant, Don, recalls,

I'm standing right there and many times they bypass me and go to someone who is not black and just assume that that's the one who's in charge; just not even ask and just assume. I just sit there and nine times out of ten my crew members will say, "Well, you have to speak to Don," or "He's the A" or whatever the case may be. I just want to just take a pie and squish it in their face. Even pilots, the same way. I'll be standing at the boarding door, you know, "How you doing?" and they keep on going and not even introduce themselves, like "Hey, I'm such and such," and it happens enough to where it's noticeable and then they walk pass you and go, "Well, who's in charge?" . . . You have a lot of people who when you speak and say, "Hey, how you doing?" they just keep on walking and don't even think anything of it.

Similar to the aforementioned experiences of black flight attendants, Don experiences a level of exclusion that reifies the racial and gendered hierarchy on the aircraft. While males are often given unmerited favor in female occupations, this is not the case for African American males. Being black and male in this case removes the power associated with masculinity. Combined, these characteristics render black male flight attendants invisible. Equally important are the actions of the pilots and other airline personnel and their open treatment of Don. The broader cultural understandings of social power and privilege openly contribute to the normative nature of these interactions with African American flight attendants and their white co-workers and contribute to the level of exclusion they experience. Having to experience those public interactions in which one is not acknowledged is heavy and should not be taken lightly as it pertains to emotional labor. In the context of flight attendants, black males will be treated as having less power than white women—this is different from the experiences of pilots and their gendered male occupation. Through systemic sexism, males have been granted a particular position of authority, even when they are in environments that are heavily gendered. This is one of the reasons Hochschild includes in her desire to study flight attendants. In providing a justification for studying flight attendants in her earlier work, Hochschild states,

> The choice to study flight attendants was also good from the point of view of understanding the relation of gender to jobs . . . To study secretaries is to study almost only women; to study pilots is to study almost only men . . . The male flight attendant, however, does the same work in the same place as the female flight attendant so that any differences in work experience are more likely due to gender . . . In many studies, the problems of women as workers are confounded with the problems of being in a minority in a given occupation. In this work at least, the shoe is on the other foot: males comprise only 15 percent of flight attendants. They are the minority; and although being part of a minority usually works against the individual, this does not appear to be true in the case of male flight attendants. (1983:15)

As she examines the experiences of white male flight attendants more in later chapters of her work, here it is important to recognize that these interactions with co-workers while on the job are not seen as "work." For these African Americans, however, it is seen as work, as they discussed much of this when discussing "the job." Those white males included in Hochschild's work do not account for the interconnectivity of being a numerical minority and being a member of a racial-ethnic group, nor do they account for the historical position of subordinate status forced on African American males. Even being in a minority status as male flight attendants, they are not always granted the authority of their white male counterparts. Consider these divergent experiences through an account provided by a female flight attendant in

Hochschild's work with the experiences of a male flight attendant in these more current interviews.

> I told a guy who had a piece of luggage in front of him that wouldn't fit under the seat, I told him, "It won't fit, we'll have to do something with it." He came back with, "Oh, but it's been here the whole trip, I've had it with me all the time, blah, blah, blah." He gave me some guff. I thought to myself, I'll finish this later, I'll walk away right now. I intended to come back to him. A flying partner of mine, a young man, came by this passenger, without knowing about our conversation, and said to him, "Sir, that bag is too big for your seat. We're going to have to take it away." "Oh, here you are," the guy says, and he hands it over to him. (1983:178–79)

In contrast, here is the narrative of an African American male flight attendant with a similar experience with luggage:

> I had one lady who was traveling internationally, and she was one of the last few to get aboard the airplane and we didn't have any more space. I mean I even used the closets that I have . . . She argued up and down for about at least five or six minutes about how she wasn't going to check her bag, and this started in the aisle. She was holding up the boarding process, and I finally said, "Ma'am, come out, bring your bag out of the aisle here to the jet way so we can talk." I don't want to embarrass them, so I kind of bring them out where they are away from everybody. At that point, once I had her out in the jet way letting her know that there's no space at all for any carry-on bag—as you can see this line right here behind you everyone's having to do the same thing. "Well, I bought my ticket five, six months ago, I should have space." And I was like, "Ma'am, I understand where you're coming from and I'm not trying to go out of my way to not accommodate you, but at this point the only thing we can do is check your bag. Or the other option you have is to stand-by for the next flight where you may be able to be accommodated with your carry-on bag, but at this point we have to check your bag." This lady was persistent; then it finally got to the point where I had to just basically say, "Ma'am, at this point the conversation is over. The option you have is either catching the next flight or checking your bag," and I just went on to the next person.

There are key differences in what it means to be a male in this "female space" versus what it means to be a black male in this space. As much authority in any given situation is offered to males, simply because they are men, this is not always granted to African American males. In the example provided by the male flight attendant here, this female passenger continued to argue and challenge his authority to the extent that he recommended she take another flight. Though many females, much like those included in Hochschild's work, experienced similarities when it came to authority or a lack thereof, so did those African American males. In essence, white males are granted the authority associated with masculinity in feminine occupa-

tions, yet black male flight attendants are in ways emasculated through the
constant negotiation process between themselves, passengers, and co-workers. The position African American males occupy as subordinate group
members indeed translates to how they are seen and challenged on the aircraft. This inequality in what it means to be black male flight attendants is a
significant aspect of emotional labor and the necessity to maintain a sense of
professionalism.

In addition to a lack of recognition of authority in these interactions on
behalf of passengers and co-workers, many of the flight attendants also experience a level of exclusion when looking at the relationships between co-
workers. Recall the earlier account provided by a male flight attendant about
how there are those times when he says, "How you doing?" and receives no
response from his co-workers—in this case, pilots. Connected to a position
of power, many of these pilots reify their perceived superior position by
openly denouncing the significance of these African American workers. In
this next section, I examine another aspect of work that is not usually considered a part of the job but nonetheless influences the manner in which subsequent work is conducted.

SLAM-CLICKERS AND HARLEM BASHERS:
THE POLITICS OF EXCLUSION

When dealing with co-workers, the idea of being invisible is one that was
noted by flight attendants and pilots alike. Though manifested in a variety of
ways, one such way this occurs for flight attendants is through the failure of
co-workers to acknowledge their presence and/or their positions of authority
when flying in the lead position. Most flight attendants in this project easily
recounted cases in which they were blatantly ignored by co-workers as well
as passengers. In some of these cases, the emotional consequence derived
from the alienation of invisibility is apparent. In addition to the failure to
recognize their positions of authority, African American flight attendants
also find themselves experiencing alienation and exclusion by being blatantly
ignored by their co-workers. Take, for instance, the example provided by
Melissa (Mel), a flight attendant for a major airline, as she recounts a recent
interaction with a co-worker.

> A couple of days ago we were leaving Pittsburgh, and they had had ice prob-
> lems so earlier flights had been delayed. When we left the hotel there were
> three sets of pilots, including the pilots who were taking us back, and three
> flight attendants, and you know I'm the only black flight attendant on board
> and there are two pilots in the back and a flight attendant in the back, and the
> flight attendant was just talking and she told this one pilot, she just asked him
> something and he started, "Yeah, I commute from Dallas," and I turned around

and I looked at him and I said, "Oh, I commute from Dallas," and he just looks at me and doesn't say, "Oh, yeah, tough commute?" Nothing, he just looks at me, didn't say anything, didn't respond.

    I hate to harp on it and say it's race but that's the only thing I can think of . . . Because I mean he was talking to the white flight attendant, no problems, and when I turn around and say "I commute from Dallas" he just looks at me, doesn't respond or say anything, and I'm like okay, the only difference I can see is that she's white and you're talking to her and I'm black and when I make a comment to you, you just look at me.

    Some of them tend to just totally ignore you. For example, we were on a 757 and there were four flight attendants, I was the only black one. We were all sitting in the middle of the airplane by the two left door; we were sitting, pilot comes on, introduces himself, looks at every white flight attendant, totally ignores me, and I say, "I'm Mel, by the way," and he just kind of looked at me funny and kept on with his briefing. Now I've had that happen more than once.

It is important to note that interactions such as this one by Mel happen before passengers even began to board the aircraft. Also important in this interaction is that Mel has an awareness of her invisibility. Moreover, as Mel recounts, accounts such as this are often experienced in front of others as though there is a blatant disregard for her presence, leaving her to deduce that this is based on her racial identity. In this one conversation, she easily recalls two examples out of many in which she was ignored. In terms of emotions and emotional labor, the consequence is that she expends both time and energy deflecting the demoralizing experience of being ignored in front of her co-workers. The significance of this event is apparent in the way that she, like many others, can recall specific cities, environments, and reactions of others. She goes on to note, "Like the incident I was telling you about, and I said 'Oh, I'm Mel, by the way' and they [the flight attendants] just kind of looked at the pilot . . . okay . . . did you not see her? I even had one flight attendant even make a comment . . . she's like, 'He acted like he didn't see you.' 'Yeah, he did act like he didn't see me.'" Important here are that those other flight attendants, all witnessing these interactions, commented to Mel *after the fact* and not to the pilots that failed to acknowledge her, causing her to relive the process of being blatantly excluded.

    Several flight attendants noted that they were not acknowledged by their co-workers and that this sometimes happens in front of others. This public act serves as a method of alienating those African Americans on board the aircraft. It is similar to the alienation faced by the African American pilots discussed in the previous chapter. In many ways, their experience is that of an outsider-within—they must simultaneously perform their job in a space they are not fully allowed to be a part of. The invisibility experienced in reference to authority is extended to include the invisibility imposed on them by others, namely co-workers. This creates an environment that is not only alienating but also serves as a larger mechanism of symbolically excluding them from this white space. The fact that they are excluded by passengers *and* co-workers should be factored into the existing theories on emotional labor and emotional display.

One other area that must be included in theories of emotional labor performed by flight attendants is the labor they must perform once off the aircraft. Though the workday has officially ended, layovers are also a time when there are often extensive interactions with co-workers. For many flight attendants, the ability to relax after a day of constant interactions with passengers and co-workers is often hindered by the knowledge that this is also another area in which they are excluded. As noted by many of these flight attendants, many of their co-workers are "slam-clickers." Slam-click, in this case, represents the recognizable sound of the hotel room door slamming and locking as though they are in for the evening. However, as many flight attendants discover, "They went out to eat, didn't ask me to go. They went to have drinks, went to the movies, didn't ask me to go, and then the next morning they ask me, 'Oh, how was your layover? This is what we did.' They call everybody but then don't call me." Most all flight attendants (and pilots) noted that on morning conversations after a layover the common question is, "What did you do?" This is usually followed by a detailed description of what "they" did and is done in a manner that leaves no room for speculation. They were not included.

Another flight attendant describes a time in which she offered to take another flight attendant's room because of smoke allergies, and she goes on to state,

> I decided to go get something to eat and as I was leaving my room I saw her and another flight attendant coming back from getting something to eat. And I was like, wow, they didn't even invite me to come with them. And I gave her my room! You know I was like, damn. You know there would be trips that I'd fly on and we have a long layover, we get to the hotel and then nobody would call but the next morning, they're all like "What'd you do? We did this." They did stuff together.

In these accounts, black flight attendants are well aware that their co-workers excluded them. This larger pattern of exclusion contributes to the atmosphere on the aircraft in that they often feel alone and as though they have no one to socialize with. Consider these instances, coupled with passenger and other airline personnel interactions, and how these experiences influence not only the amount of emotional labor that is performed throughout any given day but also how this influences how the job itself is performed. The experiences based on racial and gender identity are not factored into how these flight attendants perform emotional labor.

As but one aspect of social life and social interactions, these flight attendants deal with the exclusionary methods of their white colleagues on and off the aircraft. The cumulative nature of these interactions contributes greatly to the volume of emotional labor performed by these flight attendants of color. I have noted some of the many exclusionary methods practiced by white co-workers, but they were not limited to being excluded and/or being ignored on layovers. One primary method of alienation is found in the immense quantity of racial and/or cultural insensitivity encountered.

White perceptions about people of color or minority group members and dominant white ideologies guide interaction on the plane for African American flight attendants, and this becomes another component of their invisibility and exclusion. Similar to the accounts of pilots, these flight attendants often encountered a level of insensitivity from their co-workers in their regular conversations. Take, for instance, the following example provided by a senior female flight attendant:

> I remember sitting, you know how you land and have a few minutes of sit time before you turn that plane around, and, um . . . this white pilot just decided he wants to chat: "So, where you from, Michelle?" I said, "I'm from New York." "Where in New York?" "Harlem." He said, "Wow, nothing ever comes out of Harlem but basketball players."[14]

This comment was one with racial meanings. The deeper connection here between race, geographical location, and sport is but one aspect of a larger racial understanding of the skills and expectations of black Americans. Nevertheless, the pilot did not consider how this commentary would affect Michelle. In this particular example, the conversation and interaction was public, and Michelle was placed in a position to have to manage her emotions and the emotions of those around her. Noting that nothing ever comes out of Harlem except basketball players is a failure to acknowledge her immediate position in the airline industry as well as her human worth as a woman from this environment. In this particular case, she was left with the all-too-familiar position of many African Americans in their professional and personal interactions with whites. Many often find they are in the position to "school whites" on their often incorrect racialized assumptions. In this case, Michelle said, "I said, 'I beg to differ.' And I just started naming; I said, 'Out of six kids we have a school teacher, a doctor, a lawyer, engineer, dadadadada—I said I was an accountant, I just went on and on and on . . . '" A clear message of exclusion, interactions between flight attendants and their co-workers were often based on this level of racial insensitivity, with whites failing to be reflective about their own privilege. Truly, many whites do not *have* to see the full implications and meanings of their comments. In another case, a flight attendant recalled a recent insensitive conversation with a co-worker.

> Just the other day, we were looking at the back of this candy or something that was sold in [another country] and it had like . . . the lady on the back, she looked black but she was from like . . . you know, another country with a darker descent, a darker complexion, and I said, "Oh, this is owned by this person"—I said, "I wonder if this is the person who owns it," and she [a white female flight attendant] said "Uh, how about the person that's picking it . . . picking the stuff to make it!"

These conversations with co-workers involving racialized language and imagery are often done in a way that reiterates black feelings of alienation. As many were done directly, there were also those cases in which this insensitivity spilled over into discussions of other groups that made these African American flight attendants uncomfortable. Like the African American pilots in the previous chapter, discussions of other oppressed groups left them with a deeper perspective that caused them to wonder what the topic of discussion would be if they were not there. For example,

> There are those times where members of the crew will talk about other races of people or other groups. Like this one time we were in the van in Florida and the pilot turns around and says, "So how many gays were in the back?" I'm thinking that this is inappropriate at work. For all he knows, I could have a gay brother. Better yet, he doesn't know my status. I said, "Excuse me?" He says it again, "This is the gay capital of Florida; how many gays did you have in the back?" I said, "I don't know what you're talking about." The reason I said that is because I feel like if I wasn't in the van, his question might have been, "How many niggers were in the back?" That's how I felt based on the way that he said it.

There is a larger understanding on behalf of these African Americans that discriminatory comments directed at others can easily be directed toward them. The consequences of these conversations between flight attendants and co-workers serve as a constant reminder that in performing the job there remains a rift between job performance and being recognized as appropriate for performing the job by their co-workers and passengers. Also of importance in this interaction is the comfort of the pilot in making such an inappropriate comment to those around him. This suggests that a normative aspect of the work environment is one that recognizes the social power and privilege of white heteronormativity. Those not fitting this ideal are barred participation and, in many ways, are relegated to the margins. The implications of emotional labor in these many interactions should not be taken for granted but understood as a collective experience in which outside factors contribute to how emotional labor is performed.

CONCLUSION

For flight attendants, a large portion of the job is spent interacting with passengers and co-workers in close quarters. In recalling the accounts provided in this chapter, the connections with the spatial aspects of racist expressions and the more general connections to the structural nature of racism should also be encompassed in the emotional labor literature. Many of the interactions that take place between African American flight attendants and white passengers and company personnel originate from the broader framing of black positions, intellect, and bodies. Though there is indeed greater diversity within the ranks of flight attendants, especially when compared to the African American pilot population, there still remain significant barriers to gaining full inclusion and acceptance on the aircraft. Whether introduced through interactions with passengers or with co-workers, these black flight attendants are also reminded that a disconnect can sometimes occur when addressing their acceptability in the white space of the aircraft.

Extending the notion that the flight deck remains largely a white (male) space should encompass the idea that the aircraft itself as well as the job of flight attendant is in many ways also largely connected to the ideology of a white (female) space. White framing of blacks as being in inferior positions or "not belonging" becomes evident through the various ways flight attendants interact with one another as well as with passengers. On the other hand, flight attendants, while spending much of their time with passengers, also deal with blatant racist expressions that reaffirm the position of flight attendant as one reserved for and performed best by whites. In the above cases, flight attendants experience contradictory expectations from passengers. On one hand, they are seen as "servants," while on the other, they are denied the ability to perform a large aspect of the job they were hired to do in providing good service. Situated in the larger ideology of African American women, many of the female flight attendants here also found themselves dealing with unwanted sexual advances from co-workers and passengers alike. These accounts, like those of the pilots in the previous chapter, should be included in the literature on emotional labor, as these cases occur while in the workplace.

White co-workers often engage in the subtleties involved in racist displays by usurping authority through mechanisms of exclusion and alienation, thereby reifying the invisibility of African American flight attendants. Though many white males in Hochschild's work were treated with an elevated sense of authority based on their masculinity, this was not always granted to the black male flight attendants in this project. How our identities intersect and interact with the environment contributes to the performance of work and emotional labor. Though considered by some to be outside of the scope of work, layovers and down time between flights were also included when these flight attendants discussed their jobs. There was a level of racial insensitivity toward these flight attendants as well as a level of exclusion that was not always apparent to their co-workers. This should also be situated in the context of larger U.S. society and how our history of racism and sexism, as well as how the constricting environments in which these workers perform labor, influence these interactions. All of these elements must be considered in theories of emotional labor.

In the existing emotional labor literature, there is much information on how notions of gender and race contribute to the performance of emotional labor. But one key difference in examining African American flight crews is that there are racial and gendered images associated with particular positions as well as with members of particular groups that are contradictory. In the larger society, due mainly to systemic racism and sexism, these crew members find themselves in racialized and gendered positions in which they do not fit. This often elicits an emotional response of abject resistance on behalf of those viewing them. Note, too, that African Americans as a group have historically and contemporarily faced significant negative stereotyping and framing that carries over into how others perceive them. To move into a deeper analysis of emotional labor and emotions, it is important to show how underlying, larger structural processes influence smaller, everyday interactions. In chapter 4, I seek to situate emotional labor within the framework of systemic racism and the white framing of black Americans and also show that much of the emotional labor they perform is in direct response to those around them and is in addition to the normative emotional expectations contained in work.

Chapter Four

Emotional Labor and Systemic Racism

The experiences of black flight crews in the airline industry provide a unique lens through which to view the structural mechanisms in which racism and sexism operate, as well as the deeper connections with performing emotion work and emotional labor. In the previous chapters on black crew members, I explored how the underlying connections between racialized and gendered experiences and systemic racism/sexism contribute greatly to those aspects of the job that are undervalued and underanalyzed. In their daily experiences in the workplace, the concept of emotional labor and what is within the normative expectations of what it means to be a pilot or flight attendant do not fully capture the amount of emotional labor that these professionals *actually* perform. Using their collective experiences as a backdrop in the previous chapters serves as an introduction to the intersectionality of systemic racism/ sexism and emotional labor, and how these concepts form a maze through which the actions of white actors and the experiences of black flight crews are all intertwined, and through which these people have to navigate on a day-to-day basis. The actions whites take to maintain social power and privilege in this environment and the power removed from black flight crew members to engage in aggressive counternarratives are a part of the conundrum created by systemic and color-blind racism and those company expectations of emotional labor. Indeed, I showed in the previous chapters that emotional labor encompasses more than those interactions with passengers, but it is also inclusive of the daily interactions with co-workers. Note, too, that organizations hold responsibility by enforcing emotional labor standards. Also significant in emotional labor is the amount of *cognitive* labor performed by black flight crew members.[1] As mentioned in earlier chapters, the amount of time and energy expended to develop an effective counternarrative is cognitive labor that involves both thinking through and conceptualizing negative interactions as well as developing a satisfactory way to respond within or outside of the boundaries of the organizational norms and culture. In essence, cognitive labor is continuous in racialized and gendered workplaces and produces some form of emotional labor.

In this chapter, I introduce a broader social science theory of emotional labor and seek to fill the gap between emotional labor and the specific contexts in which workers perform it. The airport and aircraft, along with the uniforms and positions of pilot and flight attendant, are but pieces of a broader system that make up the spatial reality of racism and sexism. Before (and arguably after) the civil rights movement and the legislation that followed, hegemonically African Americans were those not capable of performing particular types of jobs within the airline industry because of deep-seated racial framing of African Americans as inferior beings. In order to create a more inclusive theory of emotional labor—one that fully incorporates the weight of emotional labor, how it is performed in various environments, and how social identity contributes differently to how and when emotional labor is performed—we must keep the many previous examples from earlier chapters fully in mind.

SYSTEMIC RACISM, RACIAL FRAMING, AND EMOTIONAL LABOR

Black flight crews are faced with the difficult task of managing their emotions and the emotions of others they come into contact with. Outside of this emotional labor, there are those expectations provided by the company and passengers that dictate and confine the methods in which emotions are performed. For instance, in their research on pilots in the airline industry, Hansen and Oster (1997) note that "the most effective flight crew performance is associated with captains who exhibit both high achievement, motivation, and interpersonal skill. The least effective crew performance is associated with captains who are below average in achievement motivation and have a negative expressive style, such as complaining" (145). These dimensions of personality as developed by psychologists place African Americans in the position of limiting their complaints against racist and/or sexist expressions and discriminatory actions by those they are in close contact with. Even as this method of self-inventory has been used by several airlines and military personnel to determine successful flight crew members, many of those participating in this project went against this idea of limiting complaints and challenged white expressions, but they often did so within the cultural boundaries of the industry.

EMOTIONS IN WHITE SPACES:
EMOTION NORMS AND WORKPLACE FEELINGS

There is a contextual reality to emotions and emotional labor that we should not separate from the institutional processes that govern them. Here, I juxtapose emotions and emotional labor within the confines of historical and contemporary white spaces. In these contexts, there are emotion norms that have developed, and the structural organization of these institutions has allowed them to persist. In her extensive work on emotions, Peggy Thoits (2004:360) notes that feeling norms "indicate the range, duration, intensity, and/or targets of emotions that are appropriate to *feel* in specific situations." With the performance of emotional labor, Hochschild (1983:56) conceptualized feeling rules as guiding "emotion work by establishing a sense of entitlement or obligation that governs emotional exchanges." Together, feeling and emotion norms are embedded processes that are subject to rules and control. Thoits (2004:360) provides a deeper understanding of the contextual significance of feeling norms, and posits:

> Because emotion norms (like all norms) are social constructions, they will vary in content over time, cultures, and contexts, both reflecting and sustaining the social structures in which they develop. . . . Because emotion rules (like all rules) are learned, children and adults undergo emotional socialization and are subject to pressures to conform. . . . Because individuals are motivated to seek approval and avoid sanctions, they will hide, transform, or otherwise manage emotions that occasionally violate emotional expectations. . . . Such efforts at emotional conformity have social consequences . . . Because some individuals fail to obey emotion norms, "emotional deviants" will be labeled, stigmatized, and subjected to social control, or under some conditions, they may become agents of social change.

As some social science literature continues to examine specific feeling rules, norms, and emotional expectations, much of the literature treats the context of emotion norms and rules as contemporary manifestations of difference, not as a result of long-standing *structural* inequality. For instance, as feeling rules and expectations vary by race and/or gender, it should also be contextualized that these perceived differences are a direct consequence of systemic inequality. Indeed, the gendered component of emotions and feeling rules have become a part of workplace assumptions, placing women largely in positions to do "people work" in part "because of existing assumptions about men's and women's emotionality: specifically, that women excel in emotional labor calling for the suppression of negative emotional displays and the presentation of positive emotions, while men are better suited to the opposite."[2] These costly social constructions of gender and racial-ethnic differences continue to shape organizational hierarchies, with minority groups

unjustifiably in lower-level positions, such as those in many service industries. Only recently has social science literature begun to incorporate how
emotions and feeling rules differ by racial-ethnic identity in a variety of
settings.[3]

Acknowledging that there are feeling norms in particular workspaces,
such as institutionally white spaces, calls for a deeper analyses of these
norms by first understanding the spaces in which they develop. In this, the
acuity of normative feeling rules is governed by well-established hegemonic
ideas of white, middle-class male and female emotions. In her work on
emotional labor in professional settings, Adia H. Wingfield (2010) introduces the idea that emotions and emotion norms created in many white
settings have developed within a culture in which white, middle-class norms
dictate this normativity. For black professional workers in this setting,

> the racial dynamics of the workplace (and of the larger society) make it more
> difficult to adhere to the feeling rules that are equally applied to workers of all
> races; and perceived that black workers are held to different emotional stan-
> dards than their white colleagues . . . Instead of being neutral, black profes-
> sional workers experience feeling rules as largely racialized in ways that con-
> strain their available avenues for emotional expression.[4]

The idea here is that some emotional expressions are deemed inappropriate based on the *actor* performing the emotion, not necessarily the emotion
itself. In many professional and historically white environments, such as the
flight deck and aircraft, the emotional expressions of anger and frustration
are often granted to those whites in positions of authority, but African
Americans in these environments note they are not to show anger under any
circumstances, leading to the idea that some emotions are marked for "whites
only."[5] In spite of the insidious experiences African Americans face in white
workspaces, when they represent only token numbers there are restrictions
on how emotional labor is performed as well as how and when emotions are
readily displayed.

ANGRY BLACK PEOPLE:
STEREOTYPICAL NOTIONS OF BLACK EMOTIONS

As I mentioned in the earlier accounts of African American flight crew
members, they encounter both blatant and subtle racism and sexism that
contribute to emotional expressions of anger and frustration. Yet within the
confines of the aircraft, they are prevented from expressing anger, though
that is the emotion they directly experience. Take, for instance, the following
account by Darnell as he discusses the emotion of anger and frustration:

> I try to voice my opinions and give my information in the calmest way that I can because I don't want them to think that I am the angry black man and be afraid 'cause then they will tell on me. White guys will tell me, "You can't present yourself as the angry black person." If you are not just accepting how everything is—everything they do, everything they say, everything that's American, i.e., white—and you speak about it too much then you remind them of what they see on TV. You are just angry—angry for no reason.

Martin noted a similar encounter with expressing emotions such as anger.

> You can't be seen as having angry black man syndrome.
> [Which is what?]
> Some people take greater offense if they've never been told to do something by a woman or a person of color. And since our industry is mostly white, there are a lot of white people that's never been told what to do by a black person. And so you tell them what to do and they question it and it's not really their job as a First Officer to question everything you do . . . and then you realize they're not questioning it because your decision making is bad, they're questioning it just because you're black . . . Even when they are wrong you can't be angry. Because what are the passengers gonna expect from you when you confront someone like that? They're gonna think that oh, sooner or later the head is gonna shake, the fingers gonna point, you gonna start showing black angry tendencies. And then you might actually scare the passengers 'cause now you're a black angry man; even though you're not even six feet tall, you've completely overshadowed everybody and they get scared so.

In these two accounts, both of these male pilots understand the implications for expressing anger in the workplace. Often faced with the all-too-familiar racial perspectives of their white colleagues (not to mention passengers), they are hindered by the societal reputation of being black and expressing anger. Even in these cases, these pilots understand that there is an explicit connection with black male anger and "danger," and these pilots connect this with the stereotypical notions of black masculinity. In these cases, whites are granted the freedom to question and attack these pilots, but many of these black pilots have learned through a variety of sanctions that their voices, frustrations, and cases of ill treatment are not heard or valued. Note, too, that white pilots have even gone as far as to state that "you can't present yourself as the angry black person," showing the pervasive nature of this faulty stereotype of general black anger. Even though this particular quote was spoken to a male, an angry black *person* is inherently inclusive of African American women and emotions.

Because emotion norms do not explicitly acknowledge or factor in social identity and status, whites attempt to reify their beliefs about African American emotional expressions. These negative emotional ideologies are not limited to black males, but there is a gendered component when examining the differences between male and female flight crew members. For instance, one female pilot noted, "I have to suppress my emotions when I am flying with someone that is a jerk. I always try to play the very safe card. That's how I am at work. I cannot be that black female that's very vocal."

One can imagine the cognitive emotional aspects of suppressing emotions of anger against racial affronts and the emotional labor that accompany these events. These flight crew members often note that though they experience anger as a real and appropriate emotion, they are not granted the ability, like their white counterparts, to openly express anger even when they feel it is justified. As part of the normative structures of the aircraft, whites have a normative ability to openly and often angrily discuss the various problems they have with people of color without fear of verbal or managerial retaliation. This suggests that in these white spaces, because they are developed and maintained as such, those that counter this perspective are seen as the problem—not the racist or sexist expressions of the actors. This raises the significant question—in institutionally white spaces, are racism, prejudice, and discrimination normative? Consider that many whites (passengers and coworkers) openly and freely express their negative ideologies of African Americans, as well as angrily argue against black entry into the industry, without institutional consequence.

Many of the comments in the pilots' accounts herein suggest an awareness of the many negative stereotypical images of African Americans and positive narratives about whiteness found in mainstream society and in the workplace. Here, these ideologies prohibit these black flight crew members from expressing anger for fear of serious reprimand. One aspect of white framing places people of color, specifically African Americans, in the position of dealing with the negative stereotypical imagery surrounding them as dangerous. Through the mainstream media and other socialization agents, the ideology of black anger as problematic and pathological has persisted and infiltrated the workplace and other public spaces.

Recall the earlier discussion of emotion and feeling norms that have developed and persisted in society and the workplace. The experiences of these black flight crew members with everyday racism place them in a position in which what they feel is contrary to what they are allowed to show. In developing this further, I suggest that *racism* and the expressions of racism in these white spaces are aspects of the normative structure of this particular work culture and environment. In these cases, African Americans are seen as "the problem," not the highly discriminatory actions of white actors. Anger as an emotion is largely connected to masculinity and masculine jobs, but anger and the ability to show it is limited to white males in the workplace, not African American males within the same space.[6] African American emotion norms in this environment involve *suppression* of anger for fear of retaliation. Peggy Thoits terms those who fail to comply with emotion norms "emotional deviants"; being such a deviant in these settings is a much bigger problem for these African American flight crew members.[7] Even when complying with conventional emotion norms, their very presence is seen as an anomaly in this space. Therefore, their emotions and their identity as black Americans are frequently outside of the normative structures of the airline industry, causing many emotions attached to them to be seen as deviant emotions. Consequently, this reaffirms the aircraft as a white space and the manifestation of white discrimination as normative. Those who go against this ideology are punished, not racism. In this space, whites (not people of color) have the institutional wherewithal to develop emotion norms deemed appropriate for African Americans—those emotions being passivity, conformity, and deference.

THE CONSEQUENCE OF ANGER

When placing this in the perspective of emotional labor, African American flight crew members have come to understand (but not necessarily accept) that racism and/or sexism is a part of the job. This is not to state that they are in agreement with white racist or sexist expressions, but they are aware of the costs of speaking up against it. Take, for instance, the following account by a young pilot, Michael.

> You know, I've been evolving. I remember the first experience I had with racism. I pretty much told him how I felt about it. And a lot of them [captains], especially with race . . . you can't deny you got the race factor, you tell them how you feel about it, well, you have to take into account that they aren't used to hearing it, they're used to kind of barking out some of it but they're not used to getting some of it back; even though it's not disrespectful or anything . . . you not cussing anybody out or anything or yelling or anything. But they don't take too kindly to you telling them anything.
>
> I remember the first experience I had with that. I told the guy how I felt about it. And at that point he tried to apologize: "I thought about it yesterday and I was wrong," and I said, "It's cool" . . . We finally got it kinda worked out where I was like all right, put it all aside and start over from here. At the end of the trip we kinda said, "Hey, sorry about everything," shook hands, let bygones be bygones, just kind of all is said and done. I thought all was said and done, but a few weeks later I get a notice to appear to the chief pilot's office and to bring a union rep because it might result in termination. And so I'm like, what can this be about? What did I do, okay, who did I fly with? I'm really pissed off, so I'm thinking, thinking, thinking, and I'm thinking John . . . no, I mean we got into it but he pretty much agreed that everything was cool . . . Sure enough, when I went to go talk to the chief pilot, and he asks me why I think I'm here, and I told him. And to make a long story short, they just called me in to find out my side of the story and find out what happened and to tell me how *I* can better avoid this stuff in the future.

[What exactly had that guy reported on you, do you know?]

He turned the computer screen around and he showed me the report he wrote. Something to the effect that I was not respecting the captain's authority and I was trying to undermine his authority or something like that. That is why I understand that you have to be careful of what you say . . . He said I was trying to undermine his authority and that I need to understand this is not a democracy and that I need to understand that what he says goes!

[Why do you think he took such offense to that?]

Still a lot of people, because of their own personal egos, take offense to that [telling them something back]. And I've had people say stuff like, "You're really aggressive," and I think that's kind of racist—that whole "you're acting really aggressive." You know when I get mad now days and think about telling somebody something, I just think about *all my visits to the office* and it's like, you know what, let me think of a better way to do this so I don't end up back in the office trying to explain it and why I got into it with somebody, you know. I just think about the consequences.

In this account, it is clear that frustration and anger are real emotions that are felt in performing the job when encountering those who are racially insensitive, yet they are also emotions that carry a different consequence for the African Americans experiencing them. They have come to understand, through a cognitively laborious process, that there is a cost to expressing emotion, even though many encounters call for an angry expression. One such cost is to be reprimanded even when they are speaking against racist behaviors. In this account, there was no mention of the white captain engaging in racial language being called into the office, nor was there mention that the captain would be asked what *he* could do to ensure this would never happen again. This assumption places the responsibility of managing and suppressing emotions solely on the African American pilot being offended and disrespected. This is truly a sort of *forced* conformity that African Americans contend with. Note here the social reproduction of racism and privilege in white institutional spaces. Racism and white privilege is socially reproduced at the micro level through the actions of white workers through their attacks of black flight crews, but it is also socially reproduced at the structural macro level when those higher-ups *backed up* the discriminatory behavior of whites. Important to this account is the amount of emotional and cognitive labor engaged in by this young black pilot as he navigates racist encounters in the workplace and in the visits with those in positions of authority during his numerous visits to the chief pilot's office.

In her work on emotional labor, Hochschild (1983:173) states,

When a man expresses anger it is deemed "rational" or understandable anger, anger that indicates not weakness of character but deeply held conviction. When women express an equivalent degree of anger, it is more likely to be interpreted as a sign of personal instability . . . That is, the women's feelings are seen not as a response to real events but as reflections of themselves as "emotional" women.

Moreover, Hochschild (1983:174) goes on to state,

> Given this relation between status and the treatment of feeling, it follows that persons in low-status categories—women, people of color, children—lack a status shield against poorer treatment of their feelings. This simple fact has the power to utterly transform the content of a job . . . A day's accumulation of passenger abuse for a woman differs from a day's accumulation of it for a man.

The emotional puzzle facing women in the workplace should also be applied to people of color on the aircraft, specifically when encountering racism. Much of the authority granted men in the masculine occupation of pilot is not inclusive of people of color, but it is indeed limited to white male masculinity. In these white spaces, retorts against the racial framing of black Americans is intolerable—intolerable in everyday interactions between co-workers and passengers as well as from those in higher positions of authority. Factoring in the long-standing exclusionary practices of the airline industry and the institutional structures that were in place to protect these racialized processes, a clear path of socially reproduced notions of the aircraft as "white" persists through the subordination of black emotional labor.

As Hochschild notes the differences in accumulation of passenger abuse for women and men, we must also take into account the differences for people of color on the aircraft. Foremost, much of the accumulation of abuse in the case of African American crew members is also in addition to passenger abuse. African Americans experience turbulent relations based on racial and gender identity from multiple actors: passengers, co-workers, and those in managerial positions. Indeed, for African Americans, this accumulation of emotional experiences happens simultaneously with the emotional labor expected to be performed within the context of work, and because it comes from multiple sources, the insulation of escape is thereby removed. Much like those emotions attached to women as signs of instability, those emotions of African Americans, when legitimately displayed, become avenues for reaffirming white perceptions of black hypersensitivity and instability.

MUCH MORE THAN EMOTIONAL LABOR: COSTS, ENERGY, AND CONSEQUENCES

Many of the pilots interviewed noted concerns about the consequence of speaking out too loudly against racial prejudices and discriminatory behavior. Noting that much of the contemporary nature of racism is more difficult to prove, they also note that there is much in the way of *energy* involved in filing claims. For instance, when one pilot discussed a flight he had with other pilots, he noted,

> I flew with one of the biggest assholes in the company this one time, and the thing is, I'd never heard of him, but on the way back he started talking racial questions and topics. And I just maintained, you know, guys are guys . . . We landed in Houston on the redeye and as I'm leaving, the senior chief pilot came up to the group, and he was interested to see how it went. I didn't know what was going on with the big picture at that time. And I said we had a good trip and that we did kind of talk about some of the racial implications of "why it was black pilots recently getting hired" and all this kind of junk. And I went on with my business. Two weeks later, the head of human resources calls me up: Chris filed a charge against me, said that I called him a nigger. That *I* had called *him* a nigger.
> [Was he a black guy?]
> No, he was a white guy!
> Now I write it all out, dropped it off, go in for the hearing. I had the union present, the union rep, and I had seventeen other crew members that had problems with him. And he was just sitting there and they just kept slapping him on the hand. He wasn't in any trouble.

In this account, this pilot was faced with being reported for using a racial epithet against a white male colleague. Consider the amount of time involved to contact the union, formulate a case, contact and get seventeen additional crew, attend a hearing, and await the results only to find that this person was not punished for making false claims (or for using racially derogatory language). Also here, we have to account for wages and time lost due to the time involved in formulating a case. This pilot was also subjected to the understanding that there is not a negative consequence involved in using racial epithets on the job. This resulted in more than an act of personal understanding of a lack of institutional support for one crew member; it also upheld the positions of both black and white pilots in the industry. Moreover, several crew members in this project noted that to file claims and make open complaints can mean the end of one's career in some respects. One pilot in his discussion of facing racism noted, "You can't let it depress you, you can't let it bring you down, you can't even bring it to the company's attention most the time 'cause they're not gonna understand. They're probably gonna look at you like a problem child or you're trying to start a history to file suit. So you don't even bring it to their attention." Here it is important to recall the earlier chapter on pilots, where those who spoke against mistreatment did in fact lose jobs, particularly the one pilot who, upon looking at himself in the mirror with his uniform on, knew he would never have the opportunity to wear it at work. Indeed, after speaking against mistreatment, he was "let go," confirming the social reproduction of racism and privilege through institutional enforcement.

Dealing with racism inside and outside of the workplace poses a challenge for people of color due to the systemic and persistent nature of racism in American society. For these black flight crew members, much of what is experienced outside of the job becomes a large aspect of what they face while on the job. There is no visible escape provided in this context—they cannot leave the situation, they are not supported by those in positions of authority, and they are sanctioned for speaking against racism. The tacit assumptions of white superiority remain firmly in place in this industry through the reaffirmation of white male normativity in the flight deck. Though some would say that not speaking against these racial affronts enhances the existing white structures, here it is important to showcase how racism persists in white spaces through the individual and institutional silencing (and punishing) of black voices. Here again, workplace and other social conformity in these cases is not merely a choice; it is often forced.

By outlining normative structures of feeling and emotions in the workplace, this section introduces the idea that African Americans are in the unsettling position of being "outsiders" within this structure. Represented and seen largely by their racial identity, the normative emotions provided by a (white) masculine status is not provided to these people of color, even when they occupy positions of authority on the aircraft. Indeed, not only are their emotional expressions of anger and frustration seen as a problem, truly it is them, as African Americans, and their presence on the aircraft, that are seen as the problem. In this section, it is important to clearly show that there are consequences involved when there is nonconformity to feeling rules. As we move into a broader conceptualization of emotional labor, recall how many encounters based on racial and gender identity are deeply intertwined with the company expectations of engaging in emotional labor. Also significant are the ways in which black emotional labor is hindered through the social reproduction and institutional backing of white-framed norms, workplace rules, and methods of expressing emotion.

THE EMOTIONS OF SYSTEMIC RACISM AND SEXISM

As we saw in previous chapters and in the discussion immediately above, the connections between racial experiences and systemic racism contribute to emotions and emotional labor. Historically, white institutions often present racial climates that are "replete with gendered racism, blocked opportunities, and mundane, extreme, environmental stress."[8] This environment is also complete with feeling and institutional norms that keep African American flight crew members in positions of performing emotional labor outside of what is expected when performing the job. Much of the emotional labor performed in this industry occurs in interactions between co-workers and is based considerably on racial and gendered identity. Many in this project confirm their knowledge that they understand this to be part of the job—an aspect they wish would disappear.

In this section, I introduce a deeper understanding of the emotional processes that take place in the performance of emotional labor. By combining those existing aspects of emotional labor and dimensions of systemic racism, the interconnectivity of emotional labor and identity introduces the notion that "who we are" cannot be separated from the amount of emotional labor we perform. Much of this is not considered in professional settings to account for the performance of emotional labor. Indeed, within the airline industry, emotional labor is just considered a necessary part of the job occurring between crew members and interactions with passengers. But this view misses the astonishing amount of emotional labor performed in interactions with passengers and co-workers that is based on salient racial and gender identity factors that cannot be changed. For these African Americans performing in historically white spaces, operating and performing emotional labor in a space that constantly reminds them that they do not "fit" is daunting.

EMOTIONS IN CONTEXT: THE CUMULATIVE DIMENSION

There is a *painful* reality to experiences of racial prejudice and bias in interactions in the workplace. Carving out a safe space within the confines of the aircraft is an aspect of work not granted to African American flight crew members. In addition to racist experiences, flight crew members noted that they often had the awareness that they were the *only* African American on the entire aircraft and often felt "trapped" (at thirty thousand or so feet). In this, there was this silent acknowledgment that they were alone, contributing to those feelings of isolation and alienation. This is one aspect of working in organizations in which women or racial-ethnic minorities, being underrepresented, is often taken for granted by others in these environments and in management. Even in these silent, personal observations, there is a certain amount of emotion work that takes place to prepare for the possibilities of what is to come, suggesting that cognitive and emotion work often starts *before* work. Indeed, there is a deep connection between private feelings and the performance of emotional labor that should also be included in the analysis of emotions through the process of very real cognitive labor.

Recall the daily interactions in the workplace that face African American pilots and flight attendants. Many interactions that occur in the workplace are based on preconceived notions of black Americans found within the white racial frame. The consistent interactions in the workplace, based on skin color and gender, are integral parts of systemic racism—parts that contribute to the (in)stability of workplace relationships. The emotions that are produced as a result of racialized and gendered interactions go beyond performing emotional labor as a commodity, but they should also be understood from the personal emotional labor that results from interactions based on things that cannot be changed. Much of the emotional labor performed by flight crew members involves a tacit understanding that even if their behavior is altered to reflect the dominant feeling norms and culture in the workplace, there are still those unalterable aspects that cause them to stand out.

When examining emotional labor in the workplace, it has to be understood that much of what crew members face in their interactions with passengers and co-workers cannot be viewed as a unique experience occurring at only *one* specific time. There is a cumulative emotional experience that is built into emotional labor that is based on events over time in the workplace. Consider in those interactions in the previous chapters the words of flight crews when they noted that particular situations happen "all the time" or "on a regular basis." Though each encounter represents a particular place in time, they also *accumulate* to create a distinctive experience in the workplace. Take, for instance, the following emotionally charged account by Charles, a senior pilot, as he discusses his experience with being overlooked as captain in the flight deck.

> I mean that happened [not given the paperwork] and I was like, Call him back here! Then I said, Where is my paperwork? I didn't receive any paperwork! I mean, I make them squirm . . . You are not gonna piss down my throat. This is my goddamn airplane and I *earned* the right to be here and I'll be goddamned if I'm gonna let you come here and degrade my position that I've earned.
>
> I know that sounds harsh to say and think like that but you have to understand . . . It has been *twenty years* and I have gone from being in the military to being an officer to flying jets and each step along the way has been *excruciatingly* painful.

As evidenced in this account, Charles notes that his experiences have been excruciatingly painful, suggesting that it is not only this instance that is bothersome but the entirety of those things he faced on his journey to become a commercial pilot. In perceiving that his treatment toward those deeming him invisible to be "harsh," he also directly connects this harshness to the collective racial experiences he endured throughout his *twenty-year* tenure to become a pilot. Too, in this account, there was a very real and observable aspect of pain and frustration as he attempted to personally explain to me his tactics. In stating, "You have to understand," Charles engages in emotional labor with me as a method to comfort and ease my perceptions of him, his tone, and the fact that he was pointing his fingers at me and pounding the table with his other fist. It was also a method of saying that his emotions were justified and should be heard. Though not stated, it was apparent that our discussion provided the opportunity for Charles to vent his frustrations, an opportunity not granted to him in the workplace.

Those participating in this project also discuss the connections between racialized encounters and both physical and psychological well-being. Ranging from "physical exhaustion" to replaying encounters "over and over," these flight crew members in their encounters face countless interactions based on flawed assumptions about them and their culture. As Tina, a female pilot, explains in a recent interaction with a white co-worker, "It really wasn't enough to just offend me to *sickness in my stomach* but it was like . . . there are people that in their ignorance don't know any better . . . They only know the stuff they see on television." Sam connected racialized experiences with illness in the following way:

> Seriously, I don't have time for the bullshit because I look at it and I weigh it all and I say, In the grand scheme of things, how is this going to affect my life? Are their words going to affect my life tomorrow? May I think about it maybe later, yeah, I may think about it, maybe I'll think, "I should have said this or said that," but the reality of it is, "Well, what would have been the result of that?"
>
> [Why do you think you ignore it?]
>
> You can make a big deal out of it but you're not going to beat it (breathes out deeply) . . . Well, because there's not a lot of "me" in this industry and some people are ignorant. Usually I don't have the time to worry about it. *If I really took it to heart and gave time to think about it, I would be calling in sick and hardly ever coming to work if I really took it to heart.*

In these accounts, the various emotional experiences of dealing with racialized encounters are in the forefront and can vary according to the context in which it occurs. Both encounters are representative of the emotional build-up experienced when working in white spaces. Though some encounters are subtle in nature, there is still an emotional "sting" that comes from the interpretation of events as being based on racial identity.[9] Tina and Sam also bring to light the physical connections to racially insensitive encounters. Though they believe no real harm was intended in the interaction that caused Tina to have sickness in her stomach or Sam to call in sick, the consequential effects were present nonetheless. In these cases, it is important to connect the repetitive nature of experiencing racism and the emotional consequence that follows (consider Sam's mention of weighing each event). Positions as pilots or flight attendants in this environment provides the added stress to black flight crews that result from threatened, perceived, and actual racism in the workplace, regardless of intent.[10] Moreover, much of this added stress is in addition to the often stressful nature facing frontline airline employees during the normal performance of work.

The daily and cumulative effects of racialized experiences have been conceptualized as microaggressions. "Racial microaggressions are brief and commonplace daily verbal, behavioral, or environmental indignities, whether intentional or unintentional, that communicate hostile, derogatory, or negative racial slights and insults toward people of color."[11] As mentioned in previous chapters, these racial microaggressions contribute to the daily amount of emotional labor performed by these crew members in their interactions with others as well as the amount of emotion management that results from the managing of one's own emotions in interactions. Recall, too, the interactions detailed in the previous chapters on racialized encounters. In these cases, the emotional severity of encountering both subtle and blatant racism in the workplace is to the detriment of these African American flight attendants and pilots. The severity of these experiences to crew members is also apparent in the easy recollection of specific locations in which racist incidents occur. Imagine the often silent suffering endured by these crew members when faced with racial encounters. Sandy, a senior flight attendant, discusses her emotions in the following way:

> I don't know. I don't know if they made me cry because they hurt my feelings or if I cry because I was so angry and you want to just tell them, "Shut the fuck up. I don't give a fuck. Fuck, fuck, fuck, fuck, fuck." I don't care. I get paid a decent wage but other than that I would get fired and tell you to go fuck yourself. But you can't say that, but you want to.

The amount of anger in this excerpt suggests that there is a heavy internal dialogue that takes place as a result of interactions in the workplace. The idea that she wants to say these things but feels she can't is indicative of the amount of internal angst these flight crew members face in addition to the demands of workplace emotional labor. In this account, Sandy notes that she cries yet is not sure why, but she connects crying to anger and/or hurt feelings. The reality of racism is that it is painful and takes "pieces of self" away from those having to endure it. Again, there are not many avenues available in this workspace that lend to venting. In addition to the inability to vent while on the aircraft, many of the respondents note that they usually wait until the conclusion of a trip to speak to others about racial incidents, suggesting the longevity in which black flight crew members are *forced to carry and relive racial interactions.*

POSITIVE EMOTIONS IN THE WORKPLACE:
BLACK REACTIONS TO PASSENGER INTERACTIONS

As we have clearly seen, black flight crews engage in emotional labor based on racialized and gendered interactions in multiple ways. One particular way came through the creativity in which these flight crew members chose to highlight those positive interactions with passengers and co-workers to offset the negative and often hostile interactions they had based on race and/or gender.[12] Notably, when I asked about positive incidents on the aircraft, pilots specifically identified interactions with passengers as a way to indicate that not all experiences with passengers were negative. This form of emotion work provided them with an outlet to express why they continue to endure the daily battles they often face on the aircraft and in the terminal. Not to mention, many of these crew members, specifically pilots, have dreamed of flying airplanes for an extended period of time. For example, Robert, a young pilot, recalled several encounters that stand out to him in the following way:

> But I can always go home and forget about that stuff when a seventy- or eighty-year-old black woman comes up and just tells you that she is proud of you. She doesn't know me, but they say, "Excuse me, young man, I'm so proud of you. You just keep doin' whatever you're doin'." I'll show up to work and deal with those racist folks any day just to make the woman that probably went through hell growing up—a hell I can't even imagine—just to make her smile.

This young pilot juxtaposes his racist encounters in the workplace with those of older African Americans enduring a racist past that in many ways he cannot connect to. In this, this young pilot notes that dealing with racism is worth it in reference to those who have endured many more hardships in their lifetimes. The painful reality of racism is one that connects history with contemporary experiences of racism. Robert does not discount his racist experiences in the workplace, but he notes that it is for the purpose of continuing to fight, not only for him but also for those that have come before him as well as those to come after. Another young pilot noted similar experiences the following way:

> I've had it happen, not actually on the plane, but I've actually had it in the airport where people have come up to me and shaken my hand, asked how old I was and what was my name. It's most likely men . . . It's 100 percent minorities that do that but most of them have been men, about 80 percent of the people that have done that have been men.
> [Why do you think they do that?]
> Because they're proud. They're proud to see someone of their race in an industry that is dominated by white men. And that makes me feel so proud. I had a black guy that was a veteran and he almost broke down in tears and he

just kept shaking my hand with both his hands. He was a really old guy and he said, "I remember when you weren't up there. . . . you weren't up in the front—they wouldn't let guys like us in the front. It is so good to see you up there." I was so proud, and I walked around with my chest poked out for the rest of the day.

In both accounts, there are bigger connections vis-à-vis black passengers and pilots of a shared and collective history of the reality of oppression. This reciprocal encouragement occurs in this environment because of the reality of the racial demographics of the industry and because of a shared knowledge of racism. In these accounts, passengers encourage black pilots through expressing "pride." Resistance and coping in these cases are done on both parts, through an understanding of the painful past of those elder passengers and through passengers encouraging pilots to stay strong. This gives pilots the desire and strength to endure what happens in the workplace. The idea here is that their progress is bigger than them—through individual accomplishments, black progress is something that is shared.

While conducting research on the experiences of black flight crews, respondents express gratitude toward those passengers who encourage them in their jobs. For these pilots, these small interactions contribute greatly to their emotional well-being and give them the ability, "even if only for a moment," to continue working. Much like those whites who recognize black pilots and call them out through deplaning or exclusion, black passengers also recognize them, and as one pilot notes, "make a beeline to the cockpit to shake my hand." This is an aspect of coping through the recognition that they do not experience racism alone, and this gives them the desire to continue to resist racial oppression.

THE THEORY OF EMOTIONAL LABOR REVISITED: CHAPTER SUMMARY

I suggest that the existing theory, largely developed by Arlie Hochschild (1983), should incorporate the interconnectedness of systemic racism and sexism, white framing, emotional labor, and the context of the environment in which interactions occur. Because the airline industry represents an organization in which gendered (and racialized) occupations are present, this atmosphere provides a great lens through which to analyze emotional labor, and it is within this context that emotional labor and emotion management is examined.

As defined by Hochschild, emotional labor is "labor requiring one to induce or suppress feeling in order to sustain the outward countenance that produces the proper state of mind in others—in this case, the sense of being cared for in a convivial and safe space."[13] Emotion management, on the other hand, focuses on controlling private emotions for personal benefit. Emotional labor is performed in a work setting and is directed toward others, while emotion management is performed in any setting as a part of daily life, but is usually done in private settings where there is use value.[14] In this conceptualization, there are distinct differences between emotional labor and emotion management and how/when they should be performed. In the context of work, specifically for black flight crews, they engage in various amounts of emotion work and emotional labor simultaneously.

As I discussed in this chapter, there are aspects of feeling rules and emotion norms that are specific to particular work environments. Indeed, various institutions will have different feeling rules according to their particular structure. Accordingly, emotional labor and emotion management should incorporate the typology of the work environment as one aspect of examining emotion work and labor. This will allow for a deeper understanding of emotional labor and the extent to which it is performed and regulated for and by different workers. In the case of black flight crews, the typology of the airline industry and the aircraft is one that has developed over time to structurally incorporate white normative structures of emotions and emotion performance. This contributes to the various ways in which people of color in these environments can and do engage in emotion work and emotional labor. Second, because there are preexisting emotion and feeling norms, emotional labor will be performed differently by those deemed "outsiders" because they are not within the normative "prototype" of the environment. Finally, even though emotional labor is performed within occupational boundaries and manipulated by management, this occupational environment inherently places differing regulations on how emotional labor is performed and monitored. Moreover, because this particular environment is structured around white cultural and feeling norms, people of color in these environments experience hyper regulation of emotion work—they are under the microscope of the organization and customers, but their emotion work is also regulated by co-workers. Even in occupations where people hold "equal job status," intervening factors of gender and race demand different amounts of emotional labor and the manner in which it is performed.

Foremost, emotional labor is contextual in that the environment itself calls for a specific type of emotional labor. Both positions represent gendered occupations, but they are also racialized occupations. In the case of flight attendants, Hochschild noted that males are granted a special power and authority simply because of their masculinity in a female environment and because of the social power afforded males. Pilots, on the other hand, represent a masculine occupation, but females, because of their social position as women, would not be afforded the same authority when entering this environment. Missing here is how racial-ethnic identity can increase or reduce authority and power in both occupational positions when coupled with gender identity. For instance, recall the experiences with black male flight attendants and how their authority was challenged by passengers and co-workers. This experience was altogether different from the white males included in Hochschild's analysis. In this particular environment, though they have masculinity, which provides a level of power in female occupations, they are also black males, which reduce masculine power to one of racialized difference in white female occupations. Black female flight attendants also experience differential treatment based on what is perceived as white "femininity" versus what womanhood represents for black females. There is a similarity between the experiences of black male and female flight attendants because of what gendered racism brings to interactions.

For pilots, though it is considered a masculine occupation, black males in this environment contend with gendered racism and white framing in that much of what is perceived about black identity is counter to the expectations of the job. An occupation requiring high skill sets, levels of education, and training is outside of the scope of the racial ideology surrounding African Americans as a group. Because of this, white females and African Americans find themselves faced with the added pressure of performing these duties while fighting the stereotype of pilot as white male only. Because of this, the first aspect of understanding emotional labor and emotion management should be from the perspective of understanding the dynamics and structures of particular occupations and the foundation from which they are built. In this, there are levels of social power and prestige granted or constrained based on social identity. Even though the industry has changed considerably since the 1960s through a variety of legal means, the understanding of emotional labor in particular white spaces cannot be examined as though it is void of this history, culture, and structure—for this misses the significance of the foundational and therefore structural significance that has led to the current picture.

Those African Americans that have entered this industry encounter obstacles with fitting in and fighting a system structured in a way that calls for emotional labor but also limits the methods in which this labor is performed. Coinciding with feeling rules and emotion norms, emotional labor and emotional displays are interconnected with perceived expectations based on gender and/or racial identity. These ideologies not only guide interactions but also limit the path in which emotions are expressed. As masculine identity and therefore emotions of anger are deemed appropriate in specific positions, anger as an aspect of emotion management is not a masculine expression on the job, but a white male expression. Anger expressed by African Americans in this environment is seen as pathological—not a valid emotion to be displayed in the workplace. Moreover, this leads to the idea that though feeling rules are in place, these rules are not applied equally to all. As mentioned in the work of Thoits (2004), those not adhering to the structured feeling rules of an environment are deemed emotional "deviants"; here I argue that in the case of the airline industry, even when African Americans adhere to the prescribed emotion norms that are in place, their emotive expressions are classified in such a way that is inherently attached to their identity, therefore classifying not only their emotions as deviant, but also classifying them as deviant.

There are limitations to understanding emotional labor without understanding the development of the industry in which it is performed. As mentioned throughout this chapter, there is a distinct difference in emotional labor performance in the airline industry that is a result of how the industry developed and how it is maintained. Differential feeling rules contribute to how emotional labor is performed. With different expectations surrounding different occupational positions and gender and racial identity, there is a level of power granted to some that is not granted to others. In the organization, all service workers perform some aspect of emotional labor, yet it is monitored differently. Because African Americans experience hypervisibility in this environment, their emotional labor is monitored more closely by management, passengers, and co-workers. Emotional labor should be inclusive of the labor performed on the job that comes from interactions based on social identity. It should go beyond those normative expectations of what is expected to be performed on the job in reference to specific occupations and include the vast amount of emotional labor that is also performed based on racist and sexist interactions. This type of emotional labor, much like the emotional labor sold for a wage, should be included as it is a major aspect of the job for people of color in institutionally white spaces. Emotional labor for African Americans in this environment, and many other white workspaces, remains constant, not something performed occasionally.

African Americans in this environment are subject to emotional regulation through the company as well as from their co-workers. Consider the example mentioned earlier when the young male pilot was told by a white colleague that "you can't present yourself as the angry black person," or the accounts in which passengers publicly deplaned at the sight of a black person in the flight deck. What of the case of the flight attendant being called a "colored girl" in front of all passengers on board the aircraft? There is an inherent power granted to some to control and regulate the emotions of others because the structures of the environment support it. Examples of company regulations come into play through reprimanding black employees who express that they felt "disrespected by white colleagues" by asking the question, "What can *you* do to ensure this does not happen again?" Collectively, there is more than one type of emotional labor involved in service work. There is the emotional labor apparent in dealing with consumers and there is the emotional labor performed to thwart inequality. In these environments, racism done by passengers and co-workers is rarely spoken of from the perspective that it is wrong, but to speak against it is wrong. How can one suppress feeling to produce a proper state of mind when that which causes much discomfort is your identity?

Hochschild states, "As a culture, we have begun to place an unprecedented value on spontaneous, 'natural' feeling. We are intrigued by the unmanaged heart and what it can tell us. The more our activities as individual emotion managers are managed by organizations, the more we tend to celebrate the life of unmanaged feeling."[15] With the increasing value placed on authenticity, the emergence of the opposite has "fully emerged—the managed heart."[16] Emotional labor, from interviews with black flight crews, shows that not everyone is faced with the task of managing their hearts. Indeed, some more than others manage their hearts and the hearts of those around them. In addition, even emotional expressions and how emotional labor is performed is hindered because emotional ownership has been usurped by cultural norms that grant unequal power to whites in this corporate space. What should remain a managed heart becomes a managed life. Yet within in the confines of the aircraft, these African Americans engage in emotional labor, and most do so by understanding the reality of their environments. They understand the reality of racism and know all too well how to cope with it. Through a variety of coping and cognitive mechanisms, black flight crew members engage in dialectical methods of survival—performing the emotional labor needed for work (and to keep your employment) while maintaining a sense of self.

The data gathered from crew members suggests that emotional labor is much larger than engaging in emotion work in reference to others, but it should be extended in a way that incorporates the structural boundaries in which this type of labor is performed. There is a great deal of differential emotional labor performed through an examination of the context in which emotions and the norms of display are created, structured, and maintained. Indeed, the social reproduction of racism and privilege in this environment contribute to the overarching ways in which individual actors perform emotion work through the institutional backing some versus others receive. This also allows the continual forced conformity and hyperregulation of emotional labor on workers of color in the workplace. Providing whites with impunity to act in racist ways and the institutional support this behavior receives adds another dimension to emotional labor that can be missed through observation—the added emotional labor of coping and resistance experienced by African Americans in this environment.

Chapter Five

The Emotional Labor of Coping and Resistance

There is a painful reality to experiencing and resisting racial oppression, and there is much cognitive and emotional labor involved. This form of emotional labor, often invisible and unrecognized by workers and organizations, is marginalized yet consistent. Working in institutional spaces that reproduce discriminatory behavior at micro and macro levels, one emotional consequence for workers of color is that to be a part of the organization, they have to work excessively hard to engage in active resistance within organizational boundaries. In this chapter, I extend the discussion of emotional labor as an aspect of work by introducing the ways in which African Americans perform emotional labor through resistance in order to negotiate and survive often hostile work environments. This form of emotional labor is an aspect of the job that remains hidden from view, yet it is a form of labor that results from interactions with passengers and co-workers.

In historically white spaces, African American workers contend with the added stressors resulting from both subtle and overt forms of racism.[1] Here too, we must recognize and call out the pervasive nature of racism and sexism in white workspaces and the subsequent pressures of being a minority in particular environments. These forced pressures on workers of color become a reality which they heavily rely on emotion work, management, and both cognitive and emotional labor in order to create a counternarrative in the workplace. Counternarratives and methods of resistance used by flight crews include:

1. Deconstructing white racism
2. Resistance through the defense of "others"
3. Active and planned resistance

4. Going above and beyond: active methods of resistance
5. Standing up to white racism: active resistance through denial of white privilege
6. Resistance through networks

DECONSTRUCTING WHITE RACISM

Essential to all types of resistance is the ability to deconstruct white racism. Moving beyond understanding stereotypes, African Americans also note the reality of racism, and they understand that many of the blatant methods used by whites in the past to express racist beliefs have changed to more covert forms. To formulate an effective counternarrative, black flight crew members deconstruct race and racism. Many crew members engage in a discussion of why they feel they have problems with stereotyping and racism in the workplace. One young pilot, Adam, gave the following comment concerning his recent mistreatment at the hands of a white captain:

> It's hatred . . . they don't want you to have anything. I think a lot of us need to understand that people like that—and this is *not* all white people—but some, they hate you. They have made up in their minds that they hate you. They hate everything about you. They hate you simply because you exist, and they don't want you to have anything. I mean, he's [a white captain who recently made negative remarks about him] making twice as much as I was making, he has the captain prestige, and he's the boss on the airplane. Yet and still, he hates to see me there, and it's as simple as that . . . We can give them all the facts we want, but they just hate you, they hate to see you. You can tell them that the sky is blue and if it is contrary to their racist views, they will disagree with you because they hate you. That's it.

Foremost, there is a collective understanding that racism is pervasive and exists, albeit changed in some ways. There is much emotional labor involved in resisting and coping that occurs primarily as a result of interactions in racialized and gendered workspaces and society in general. To induce or suppress the feeling of comfort in others is not always possible, nor should it be, yet African Americans engage in emotional labor with co-workers and passengers and also within their group. The emotional labor that is produced as a result of racist expression remains constant for these African Americans and is often produced through the cognitive process of conducting a cost-benefit analysis. They perform this labor to resist racism, and they perform it through the expectation that racialized encounters will occur. Note, too, the considerable amount of time and energy, through cognitive labor, used to give a careful thought analysis of the persistence of racism. There is also something to be said of the longevity of racist experiences that create a situation in which these young African Americans develop their own theories of white racism. This is not something created momentarily but developed over time through collective experience. The above quote by Adam is indicative of the amount of time given to developing an understanding of his mistreatment in the workplace. Noting that he believes the white captain hates him simply because of his existence is an emotionally troubling conclusion. Adam further notes that "you can get all the sociologists and all these psychologists and delve into the psyche of what's going on in their head. But, if you want to just keep it simple, it doesn't take a genius to figure this out . . . they [pause] just [pause] hate [pause] you!" To Adam, and many other African Americans in this industry, this simplified explanation is one reached through years of negative interactions for no other reason than their racial identity.

Thus, one part of this coping is developing a clear understanding of how, when, where, and why whites engage the racist behavior that creates the need for emotional labor and resistance. One way that African American flight crew members situated resistance was through a collective understanding of the changing nature of racism, and the systemic nature of racist expressions. As one young pilot poignantly states: "I know that racism has changed. It isn't so much in your face now . . . It's subtle, it's underneath, and it's sneaky . . . We no longer have to worry about Jim Crow. Now we have to worry about James Crow, Jr., Esquire!" This idea of James Crow, Jr., Esquire situates the façade of racial equality, available in American discourse, in the forefront. Referencing surface policy changes promoting racial neutrality, these flight crews posit that with the changing laws and discourse, it is much more difficult to prove the existence of racism. This creates an altogether different limitation—how do you fight something many deny exists? Take, for instance, the perspective of Jerome, a senior pilot of thirty years:

> In the past thirty years many things have changed on the surface. As a result of the lawsuits that happened to correct the racial imbalance, companies have tried to maintain a color-blind workforce where they try to keep race out of the equation. This is a good thing *on the surface*, but you are dealing with individuals and individuals are going to be who they are. People still might not like you based on what they see, and they might do things to negatively affect you, but then you would be hard-pressed to characterize that as something associated with race. You really have no provable foundation to say that this was racially motivated. If you did think that, say that, or suggest that, they can come back and say you are paranoid, obsessively paranoid based on race.

While this pilot notes the legal changes that have taken place over the years, he also notes that no real structural change has occurred. These surface (symbolic) changes have also introduced a new white language surrounding making formal complaints about racial discrimination. The idea of blacks as paranoid, complainers who "play the race card" (a common and white-created phrase), has become a prominent white tactic to keep African Americans in their place. In the above assessment of the situation, these surface changes in which African Americans and white women enter corporations in token numbers in no way account for the consistent institutional support of mistreatment. Through collective memories shared with other African Americans and the personal mistreatment experienced on a consistent basis, the realization that hatred is not based on anything you have done, but on who you are, is an emotional challenge requiring much time, energy, and emotional labor in the workplace.

Because of this, many forms of resistance factor in the new boundaries in which they must engage in a racial dialogue. Recall the common methods of resistance that are used by crew members and note that there are also boundaries and limitations that prevented some more than others to engage in open forms of resistance. Engaging in resistance is contextual in the sense that what can be done in the workplace is subject to the normative structure of organizations, possible disciplinary action, social stigma, and backlash. Consider the examples in previous chapters in which black flight crew members recounted the consequences of formally speaking against racism/sexism. The consequences of engaging in open resistance in many cases can have the consequence of job loss. Besides formal complaints, these crew members engage in forms of resistance that fit well within the boundaries of the organizational structure. There are situational variables that contribute to the likelihood of engaging in active resistance that often coincide with the severity of the racist incident. Subtle forms of racism are often met with subtle, micro resistance, and those more blatant forms of racist expression are often faced with active and sometimes public resistance.

RESISTANCE THROUGH THE DEFENSE OF OTHERS

Much social science research focuses on public and visible activity in resistance, yet there are many invisible, micro-level methods of resistance that are equally important.[2] Many of the more formal, institutional transformations came through legal proceedings brought against the airline industry in the late 1950s and 1960s. Indeed, most airline employees credited these black pioneers as paving the way for their ability to fly on the aircraft and/or serve as flight attendants. Though most are not pioneers in the sense of filing legal claims against the airlines, many engage in the frontline, day-to-day, more personal, private levels of resistance in their interactions with white passengers and co-workers. The difficulty of resisting racism in an environment that structurally promotes it is one cost to working in the airline industry. Here, the cost of performing emotional labor is one that is not shared equally in the industry, yet black flight crews perform it on a regular basis. In this, it is equally important to recognize the many subtle, everyday forms of resistance that occur on the aircraft.[3] Consider that "most whites are able to go to work without having to ponder deeply how to relate to others in their workplaces as one of only a few members of their own racial group."[4] In this specific environment, whites make up the racial majority of workers and are supported by a culture and institutional structure that reinforces their dominant cultural ideologies.

Even outside of what it means for passengers to see them on the aircraft, black flight crew members actively engage in resistance because of what it means to others currently in the field and also those yet to enter the industry. Consider the example provided in an earlier chapter when the flight instructor told the young black gentlemen he didn't think they would do a good job because they were black. This pilot countered this ideology and justified doing so in the following way:

> I said what I felt right there. I didn't actually need to talk to HR or talk to anybody in the office because I told the guy what I thought. He told me he liked to use the "n" word. I told him—I looked in his eyes and I told him, "Don't you *ever* in your life say that around me . . . you understand!" It was the same when he said he thought we wouldn't do good because we were black—indeed we did. So you need to change your thinking, okay . . . I confront it and move on. *I wouldn't want the guy to get fired.* He has a family to feed, but that kind of thinking is incorrect.
>
> [So usually to cope with it, you just go ahead and confront it? Why?]
>
> Because I think it's going to make a difference for the people coming behind me. He had preconceived notions, but he was willing to empty the cup once he met us and saw that we were something different. Hopefully his perception is now changed. If there is a black pilot in the hiring pool, hopefully he won't think he has to lower the bar.

In this account, as well as many others, black flight crews continuously expressed that they do think of the possible outcome of the white actor, even though they have expressed racial sentiments. This level of sensitivity, in the idea of "I wouldn't want him to lose his job," is one that is widely shared by African American crew members, even if this same sort of humanizing consideration is not granted to them. Black crew members also attempt to understand racism from an individual perspective, through their constant note that this is "not all white people." Here, an aspect of coping is done in the attempts to examine racial experiences on a case-by-case basis and not to attribute white racism to cultural pathology. This internal analysis, though seemingly brief in nature, engages emotions of a collective understanding of black experiences in white environments. To engage in both cognitive and emotional labor in this example is evident through the thought processes involved in confronting racist actions, while providing emotional labor within the boundaries of white-created and controlled ideas of "professionalism."

As mentioned earlier in this chapter, resistance in structurally white environments can carry significant costs for black flight crews. Much of the emotion work and emotional labor is invisible, yet black flight crews find subtle ways to engage in resistance through the defending of racialized and gendered "others." Because there are gendered stereotypes in place of the African American male as "aggressive and angry" and of black females as "loud and aggressive," they often engage in resistance in ways not to reify white stereotypes of them. One such way they resist racist and sexist talk is through the defending of others. In many cases, white males in the flight deck discuss other racial groups and women in a way that suggests an opportunity to bond against racial and gendered groups, yet African American pilots see this not as an opportunity to bond but as a reality of their racial and gender prejudices and privilege. In those specific cases in which whites engage in racial discussions, they counter black arguments from the perspective of being "paranoid," taking things too seriously, or the notion that they were not being serious. On the other hand, when discussing other racial groups, intent to engage in racial and gendered discussions is implicit. One young pilot uses the following method to insert the absurdity of racial prejudice:

> I flew with a couple guys who have real stereotypical views on Muslims. And I mean, I'm a Christian, but a lot of pilots—there have been two guys specifically that have been outspoken, saying that we should profile Muslims. And being a black man and going through some things coming [growing] up, I'm all against profiling. So their argument was that Muslims are the only ones carrying out terrorist acts or whatever. And I was like, "All right, that may be the case lately, or whatever, but if that's the case then we should profile all white men." They're like, "For what?" I'm like, "For being serial killers." You know? And he completely looked at me, I was like, "That's how absurd you sound to good Muslim people who are just as upset, if not more upset, about acts or things that have gone on by a few Muslim extremists."

In this particular example, as well as many others presented in earlier chapters, pilots engage in a form of defensive resistance on behalf of others. First, this is done in order to say that discrimination, in any form and against any group, is unacceptable. Second, this is done because there is an awareness that if whites hold these views of others, they are also likely to hold racist views of African Americans. For instance, when sexist and racist discussions are involved, black pilots often retaliated with "Well, men do that, too" or "This was Mexico anyway." This active resistance provides the opportunity for black flight crew members to speak up against racism and sexism of any kind, while passively introducing the idea of "That's how absurd you sound." Done in this way, black flight crews can attack insensitivity because it is not directly connected to them. It also introduces those white crew members with an inability to say that blacks are overly sensitive about racial issues. Indeed, it is harder to insinuate black paranoia when the bonding topic is not on African Americans but on other racial groups and women. Again, it is important to consider the proximity in which these pilots work with one another and the methods in which African Americans attempt to engage in discussions on race while seemingly being nonconfrontational. To do this, emotional labor is engaged in such a way as to create a counternarrative about inequality while suppressing emotion.

Even in those accounts in which white co-workers blatantly ignored white female captains in the flight deck, African Americans also used this opportunity to correct white co-workers on their behavior. Stating "I am not in charge, she is" calls out inappropriate and disrespectful behavior aimed at women. Though this is something that was not done for them by their white counterparts, black pilots spoke up against this simply because it is an injustice, even if not theirs. There is a collective sympathy to injustice, largely because of the deeply developed understanding that what is aimed at others—sexism and racial prejudice—is also usually aimed at them. For instance, in a discussion of affirmative action in the flight deck between a white first officer and captain in which a black male pilot was jump seating, the captain did not end the conversation with the first officer when the first officer stated, "You know, I was flying with this guy, and you know he was one of those guys I could tell got his job from affirmative action."[5] In this case, the black pilot spoke up:

> I couldn't help it and I had to say something. I said, I told him, I was like, "Look, obviously you don't understand, you're talking to a guy who has been through a lot more experiences than you have . . . you haven't been discriminated on because of your race. Yeah, you may think affirmative action is reverse racism, but it ain't. I don't know the guy you're talking about, but I guarantee you, he's been through a lot more shit than what you've been through. I would respect that!" At that point, the captain changed the subject (laughs).

In this particular example, the white first officer used a passive method to talk about race and African Americans in such a way to reference an entire group. The idea here that "he couldn't help it" and had to speak up also lends to the intensity of engaging in emotional labor to resist racism. For a great deal of time before speaking up, this pilot sat with his head down, weighing the costs of speaking up versus not speaking up. This requires much thought, energy, and time to have a cost-benefit analysis in terms of engaging in racial dialogues with white co-workers. Much like the pilot in this case deciding to speak against inequality, many others also resist racism in active ways. In these accounts, there is an internal discomfort, or dissonance, that arises from the mistreatment of others that produces frustration and anger. In retort to these emotional expressions, black crew members, even to their possible detriment, actively resist oppression.

Because of the way the aircraft is structured, flight attendants and pilots have different opportunities to resist racism, suggesting resistance to be contextual, much like emotional labor. Flight attendants are provided various avenues to resist because the environment is structured in a way that multiple people can observe an interaction that would otherwise be a private event. Pilots, on the other hand, often engage in racist dialogues and resistance behind closed doors, in a more private setting in which they have to contend with the "your word against mine" mentality. Much of what happens with flight attendants occurs on the "frontstage," or in front of others, making both their experiences with prejudice and resistance a public event.[6]

ACTIVE AND PLANNED RESISTANCE

Many pilots and flight attendants engage in active forms of resistance in reference to racist or sexist interactions. Active forms can be through the ideas of using racism as motivation as well as calling out racist expressions. In the earlier chapter on flight attendants, one such example of active resistance is present in the interaction in which a [white] female passenger proclaimed that she wanted to speak with the "colored girl." In this case, this flight attendant engaged in active resistance to counter the representations of her as "colored" and as "girl":

> So, I finished my service in the front and I got my lipstick on, and I went to the back. I started right there at the front of coach cabin and I looked from side to side; I walked all the way back there. And I was saying as I'm going, "Who wants to talk to the colored girl?" It wasn't no black folks on there but me. She sitting there with her arms folded, and I'm walking all the way back, saying, "Somebody wants to talk to the colored girl; who is it?" And I put my hands on my hips and I'm just kinda going along, and I get to the exit row and I said, "Somebody wants to talk to the colored girl!" I just kinda stood there 'cause I knew it was someone in the exit row. I said, "Somebody wants to talk to the colored girl; who was it?" Everybody around there had put their head down, and I'm looking at the poor lady and she kinda had her head down, but she raised her hand to say that she wanted to talk to the colored girl.
>
> I'm thinking to myself how I had not heard that saying in years. So, I look at her and I said, "Now, ma'am, before we get to what your problem is, you tell me what color I am." I leaned close to her and said, "When I smile, I'm brown. When I'm pissed off, I'm brown. When I die, I'm gonna be brown. So you tell me what color I am." I just went into this whole thing and she was sitting there like, "Oh my God!"

In this account, the flight attendant used a public forum to resist this form of gendered and racialized oppression. By starting at the front of coach cabin and making her way back to the exit row, this flight attendant involved all of those around her to point out the fact that someone used language toward her that is unacceptable. In this, she also reminds all other passengers that this is not tolerated by introducing what was done privately by one passenger to the entire aircraft. After hearing that the passenger didn't want the flight attendants in back to serve her, this flight attendant engages in emotional labor by saying to the passenger, "Don't worry, momma gonna give you a good service, just relax."[7]

There are several forms of resistance in this example. The black flight attendant resists the position of oppression by lecturing the passenger about the inappropriate use of the description "colored," yet she also relies on gendered resistance to do this. By placing herself in a position of authority (momma), she not only uses the term to note the fact that she disciplined the passenger but also that she softened this by referencing herself as mother. This form of resistance is gendered in the sense that this flight attendant relies on her gender as woman (momma) to resist the passenger's reference of "girl." It is also important to look deeply at the planning involved in this example of resistance. The flight attendant notes that she finished what she was currently doing, put on lipstick, and proceeded to walk to the back of the aircraft. Inherent in this is the idea that this flight attendant used a good deal of time thinking and replaying the incident in her head before openly confronting the behavior.

Flight attendants also relied heavily on involving others to call out racism. As mentioned by several flight attendants, there was the avoidance of whites to accept drinks from them; most flight attendants countered this by informing the other flight attendants on the aircraft that this particular passenger "does not want anything to drink." This causes those passengers who would not accept beverages from them to account for "why" they did not want a drink. For instance, Linda, a senior flight attendant, noted,

> When passengers refuse to take a drink I usually point out to the other flight attendant that that person did not want anything to drink, so we can move on. If they ask the other flight attendant for something, I usually say, "So, you didn't want anything from me?"

This causes the passengers to account for the particular behavior and acknowledge the reasons they did not want a drink from the black flight attendant. Other flight attendants rely on similar methods to resist this subtle form of discrimination. As passengers usually feel comfortable expressing that they do not want to be served by black flight attendants, flight attendants also use this opportunity to publicly call them on it or "put them on front street" about their behavior. We must look also at the emotions involved in being openly discriminated against. To be denied openly in front of others can cause significant emotional pain, and there is much time and energy included in devising plans to counter this behavior within acceptable company boundaries. This invisible emotional labor provides black flight crew members with a way to resist racism without causing too much discomfort in others. Apparent here is the consistency in which these interactions, or interactions similar to these, have occurred. Much in their methods of resisting suggests that they have had *numerous* accounts in which to consider and know how they would handle the next one.

Active resistance against racist interactions was also done in those interactions with co-workers. As many flight attendants and pilots recalled openly racist encounters with co-workers, they also spoke of the various ways to handle this. Gwen, a senior flight attendant, recalled an interaction in which pilots boarded the aircraft late during a time when flight attendants were working on getting coats from first-class passengers, and they demanded coffee (even before making formal introductions). The encounter went as follows:

> So the pilot gets on and he never spoke to me, I don't know if he spoke to Jimmy [another black flight attendant], but he never spoke to me, and then he asked Jimmy, "Is there coffee?" Jimmy said, "Well, it's not on but I'll put some coffee on." So I'm standing near the door and it was about fifteen minutes after that, and he's [the pilot] looking at me and shouted, "IS THE COFFEE READY YET!?" And I just froze right there and piercingly stared. I said, "It's still brewing YET!" and Jimmy's standing there. I said, "Jimmy, does he think I'm Kizzy?" You know, making all these remarks, I didn't do it directly to him because that's when I can get in trouble, but I'm telling Jimmy so that he can hear me. I said, "Does he really think I'm Kizzy or something? Am I on the plantation?"

In this account, the reference to Kizzy, a slave character from Alex Haley's 1974 novel and 1978 miniseries, *Roots*, is done in a way to insinuate the fact that the pilot is being demeaning in his yelling at the flight attendants for coffee. Including references to "the plantation" implicitly tells the captain that she is not in a position of servitude, even if he thinks so. This method of resistance was also done in a way as to not directly attack the pilot but allows the flight attendants to openly resist those demands by suggesting she will get him coffee in her own time. There is also a collective involvement present here as she discusses the notion of Kizzy with Jimmy, another black flight attendant. It is in this moment that both flight attendants engage in a form of resistance through the collective understanding of who Kizzy is and what this figure represents.

Flight attendants in this project often relied on active resistance to deal with racism or sexism as it happens, specifically when happening with passengers. As Gwen goes on to state, "I nip it; I usually nip it right away and it doesn't bother me after." When asked why she does this, she replied, "Just so they can be aware. I feel it's a teaching mechanism. Just in case you're ignorant of this, and don't know you're doing it, let me let you know." However, while flight crews stated they always attempt to handle these encounters in "professional" ways, they are not always very successful. In active resistance, those extreme encounters are sometime met with extreme resistance. For instance, a male flight attendant mentioned one encounter in which he says he was not professional: "A white lady said she'd spit in my face. I did say, 'Ma'am, excuse me, but if you spit in my face I'll be spitting back in yours.'"

GOING ABOVE AND BEYOND: ACTIVE METHODS OF RESISTANCE

African American pilots continuously engaged in forms of resistance in which they used racism as motivation to succeed. As one pilot notes, he does his best to perform well because "it ruins their day"; other pilots performed well to show the insufficiency in white perceptions of black skill. To engage in this form of emotional resistance, African Americans spend considerable time devising ways to counter the overarching narrative of the deficiency of black skill. As Donna, a female pilot, noted,

Well, in 2005 we had just started hiring again since September 11th, and the [white] captain, after I said hello and introduced myself, he didn't say hi back, he just started saying, "What's your background; where did you fly before this?" I said, "I was flying for the guard; I was flying C130s, and prior to that, I was a commuter captain." Then he said, "Well, the last C130 puke I flew with tried to scare the shit out of me. You know this is not a C130, right?" Now, I'm thinking, you just met me, and this is what you're saying to me. So I said, "Yes, I know this is not a C130; it's a 737 and I'm gonna go do my walk around." So, I did my walk around and I'm thinking because I was so upset, "I guess this is the kind of day we are going to have, huh?" I was upset! I came back, and he was rude to the flight attendants and he was so obnoxious. By the time we landed, none of the flight attendants were talking to him. I was the only one near him, and so I decided I wouldn't talk to him either. When he asked me any questions, I'd answer them and that was it. I didn't hold a conversation with him. When we were flying into Newark, I clicked off the autopilot to hand fly and I was very confident because I'd been hand flying the C130s. So, he starts with the loud "OH, GOD HELP US" routine; he was being a wise-ass and I'm laughing in my head as I made a *beautiful* landing. I landed and I showed him.

In this case, Donna did not let the negative attitude of the captain stop her from hand flying the aircraft but instead took this opportunity to show the pilot that his judgment of her was uninformed. Also, she took great pride in this and noted that she "laughed" in her head as she made a beautiful landing. By disengaging in the interaction, she took both an active and subtle method of resisting his racist and gendered ideology of her and other pilots. Initially, Donna recalls the negative stereotypes of her abilities and notes that she was "upset" and spent considerable time thinking of the actions of the captain. Silently engaging in emotional labor through resisting the attitudes of the captain, Donna provides a way to also provide some satisfaction to herself. Adam noted that he "shows them" by openly resisting racist ideology through skill. He states:

> That's why I outfly them and I find it comical. [I] turn that autopilot off and hand fly this bitch. I mean, when you just grease a landing in . . . man. I mean, I hand fly the hell out of a plane.
>
> And so, what fuels that? It's not fear of what someone else thinks or what my captain might think, it's because I love my job. I think each of us would tell you how lucky we are, how fortunate we are to be doing something that we love and to make a great living doing it. So we're actually very lucky, *but it comes at a high price*, and the price you pay is in the effort and the time and the determination that you all put forth. And we all do it. We all pay our own cost, we all go through our own hell to wear our wings, and now that we're here we're going to work doubly hard to make sure that we stay here. So that's the challenge.

The high cost the pilot mentioned in the above example provides clarity regarding the amount of time spent resisting racism. Here, it is also important to note that while many have the opportunity to go to work and enjoy the work they perform, it comes at a cost for black flight crew members. Much of the pleasure they seek in performing their duties is reduced through their experiences with racism and racial prejudice. Indeed, one common ideology found in interviewing black pilots is the idea that flying is something they have always wanted to do. Yet much of the desire and comfort received from obtaining goals is stolen through their negative experiences and the ensuing time spent devising strategies to resist it. To "go through . . . hell to wear our wings" is truly indicative of the struggles facing these crew members and also lends credence to the emotional energy and labor necessary to succeed.

An aspect of going above and beyond is connected to understandings of the effort and triumph it takes to make it into the industry. Because of this knowledge, African American pilots find ways to engage in emotion work to preserve the intensity and integrity of what they have worked for. In this, they resist negative interactions by preserving their overarching knowledge of what it takes to make it and what it takes to ensure that passengers and co-workers do not have the power to reduce or take away those efforts. This form of resistance is done through the protection of self and position, and pilots rely heavily on this method to resist white racism.

STANDING UP TO WHITE RACISM:
ACTIVE RESISTANCE THROUGH DENIAL OF PRIVILEGE

As noted in previous chapters, many passengers often openly exited the aircraft when African American pilots were visible. This painful reality of having others publicly leave the aircraft should be highlighted as one that is much more than a public act, for it also involves a significant amount of personal emotion management. In these cases, there is also the task of engaging in emotional labor to all those witnessing this interaction. Donna also recounts an experience with a passenger in which the passenger openly attempted to reject her position as captain.

> I have had a lot of rude comments from passengers. But this one time out of New York, I had one [white] passenger show up one night, and she saw that I was flying the plane and she didn't want to get on. So I told the gate agents, "Close the door. I'm getting out of here and she can take the Greyhound." They were getting ready to close the door and she saw that I was serious, so she got on.

In this case, Donna called the passenger on her inappropriate behavior by stating that the passenger "can take the Greyhound." This form of active resistance was one shared by many black pilots when passengers openly deplaned or refused to enter an aircraft in which they were flying. Another pilot, Tim, noted that a passenger deplaned when she "noticed" him in the flight deck. As the captain of the flight attempted to go to try to calm the white female passenger down, the young black first officer noted,

> He was going to stop her and I remember me putting my hand on him telling him, "If you stop her, *I'm* getting off this plane, too." If you try to comfort this lady that doesn't want to be on this plane because she saw me, I'm off! So, yeah, we got her off the plane and that was it.

In the accounts of Donna and Tim, both took active approaches in resisting racism against passengers. Much like flight attendants, pilots actively find ways to engage in resistance against racist expressions that are both within and outside of the boundaries of the normative culture of the industry. In these active cases, African Americans resist racism by engaging in emotional labor that allows iteration of main points and principles, but in a nonconfrontational way. In this, they engage in the emotion work of maintaining a sense of self while also engaging in emotional labor resulting from the reproduction of racist interactions. Those participating in this project carefully evaluated situations on a case-by-case basis and found it necessary to actively engage in resistance when they believed the "costs" associated with not openly resisting outweighed those benefits. In this, most noted that if blatant racism was at stake, "they had to speak out against it." In those cases in which passengers openly deplaned, black flight crew members also actively and publicly resisted this form of prejudicial treatment by openly denying access to the aircraft. In an earlier chapter on pilots, a female passenger associated the young black pilot with the movie *Soul Plane*. In return, he notes,

> So I always thought that there are white people out there that don't see us unless they turn on the TV, and that's what they see. So, she saw *Soul Plane*, and that is her perception of black pilots. Now, the alcohol brought out her true tongue, and she told me exactly what she thought of my black ass as I stood there in my uniform, on my job. And that's why she had to sober up and wait on the next plane!

Resisting racism is a process that should not be taken for granted. Those posed with the necessity of resisting racism are often put in the forefront, whereas the racist *actions* of others are relegated to the back burner. In these accounts, African American pilots use a public space to engage in emotional reactions, yet they are done within the boundaries of company standards. These crew members have to simultaneously engage in a protection of self while engaging in emotional labor for the benefit of others. Also noteworthy in these accounts is the role of gender in these racist affronts. Though it is usually believed that white women are less likely to hold pervasive racial attitudes, all cases of open deplaning were carried out by women, adding an additional component of sensitivity and complexity in engaging in emotional labor and resistance between African Americans and white women.[8]

RESISTANCE THROUGH NETWORKS

African Americans in aviation have instituted formal networks to form relationships with others in their fields. By providing comfort to those with collective experiences, these networks formed through friendships and more formal avenues present black flight crews with the ability to vent frustrations and provide encouragement to one another, and these networks also provide an avenue to "pass the word" on who to watch out for. In order to resist racist encounters, African American crew members actively seek out and engage in lasting relationships with others in the field as a method of "surviving" the industry. In this, they actively relay various tactics that provide methods of coping and resisting racism. By giving voice and validity to racialized experiences, these flight crews share examples of their experiences, and this often allows experiences to be placed in context and to provide the knowledge that they are not necessarily alone in their experiences on the aircraft. But there is also an emotional cost to these networks. By discussing the racist encounters that occur on the aircraft, these issues become bigger than individual experiences, but they serve as a method of engaging in emotional labor due to the experiences of others. In other words, dealing with racism becomes a burden for all those involved in the discussion—they, too, now carry the effects of racism, even if they did not experience it firsthand.

> My mentor is a black pilot, and he tells me that you always have to be ready 'cause they are going to always throw it at you when you least expect it. I mean, you can be at work just lollygagging and hanging around and then, out of the blue, someone makes a racist remark or will do something out of line and you weren't expecting it. So he says you have to always be ready so that you can deal with it right then and there. So I can deal with something immediately if it is serious enough. That way, I don't have to take it home and think that I should have said something. But really, it is just another day. I will call someone up and say, "Guess what happened to me at work today?" By the time I make it home, it's a joke.

Engaging in networking with other black flight attendants and pilots provide an environment in which those flight crews feel they are not being "judged" or hypersensitive. As one flight attendant mentions, after trips in which she has difficult interactions with passengers and crew members based on race, she gets with other flight attendants and "we'll just sit down and have bitch sessions, and just bitch bitch bitch bitch bitch about what's goin' on."

Successful networks also provide an opportunity to clue in other crew members on what to expect in the industry. Indeed, many note that this is more than encouragement; it is also a form of "cheerleading" used to encourage other pilots to endure those difficulties they face.

> We spent a day and a half just explaining to them [other African American pilots] different things they can expect—how to successfully go through an interview because when a question is asked, it's not even what they're looking for. It's games they play. And once you understand the mentality, it's very easy to be successful, but the mentality is not natural.

When discussing his relationship with another black pilot, Sam goes on to state,

> I was his cheering squad. I was his cheering squad. Marvin, you can't quit. You're going to make it; you're going to make it. He would send me the questions, I would ask him questions, and he'd give me the answer. "Well, you

left off this word because you got to give the answer exactly as it is in the book, word for word, not because that's required, it's because you can't give them any excuse, any excuse—you're under the microscope. Remember what I said, word for word." To this day that boy can draw a system out blindfolded, and white boys, they don't even know this—he can draw it out blindfolded and not even leave out a word. Because we used to stay up [to] two or three in the morning.

This form of bonding, often on the basis of race, is one major method used by African American flight crews to engage in a collective resistance. Acknowledging that they are "under the microscope," these crew members provide safe spaces in which to have discussions on the similarities and differences of being black in a predominately white environment. Delving deeper into the experiences of black crew members and the usefulness of forming lasting relationships also lends to the larger idea that African Americans often feel they have to "be better than" their white counterparts. By passing along methods to perform well on exams and training and on ways of hand flying the aircraft perfectly, the overarching idea here is that black crew members strive extremely hard to be the best they can be just to be seen as *acceptable.*

Messages of performing well permeate black thought in the industry. The idea of being "watched" and studied on a consistent basis caused for a continual type of emotional labor to be engaged. Performing exceedingly well at all times is a cross to bear while working in white environments. As one pilot noted, "you have to be superblack" in order to be a part of the industry. This notion of "I'll show you" comes at the great cost of always seeking perfection and acceptance based on skill, not negative stereotypes attached to their race. These methods of success and coping are passed on in these formal networks as well as from family members.

My mother and father raised me, and they grew up in the south—in Jim Crow Texas—and the way they raised us was like it [racism] was always going to be there. You were always going to have to deal with it. If you want to succeed, you had to be well above average. You know, you can't just be average—average is for them, not for us. My dad used to call it supernigga. You want to do anything in life, that's what you got to be. He'd always say, you gotta be supernigga, you gotta know everything. So to me that was just part of being supernigga; that I gotta think about how I'm gonna deal with this person when I see him at work. I had to think about it. And if I let that bother me, I need to be doing something else 'cause those folks aren't going anywhere, and they are not gonna change their disposition on the issues.

Another crew member explains it in the following way:

There's just some things that are just unacceptable and it's not contingent on him to adapt to you, it's contingent on you to adapt to him. So you almost have to be super black. You have to be flexible enough to adapt to the appropriate norms of behavior in that cockpit and then be able to revert back to what is considered acceptable or comfortable on the street corner should you remain in that environment, and many of us do. We don't turn our back on where we came from; if anything, we're looking for opportunities to grab one of them and pull them up.

In these accounts, both pilots note the necessity of being highly trained, skilled, and adaptable. The ability to survive in multiple environments is one method of coping that many African Americans engage in to survive a painful racist reality.[9] To contend that one has to strive for a level of perfection in the workplace is an aspect of emotional labor that is done to induce particular feelings of safety in co-workers and passengers, all while reinforcing a very positive image of self.

Though formal resistance has often been called upon in making significant legal and policy changes, the reality of racism indicates that the everyday reality and necessity of resistance is extremely valuable to crew members. As they understand that there is a collective need to make changes to the industry, they also note that structural norms make it difficult to formally make claims against racism. Moreover, there is a heavy cost to engaging in formal accusations that is largely missed when understanding resistance. As mentioned by several in this chapter, significant costs to speaking out against racial prejudice include being reprimanded, being labeled as a troublemaker, and the amount of time required for following through with those claims. Overwhelmingly, these crews understand this to be a "fight you cannot win." Truly, in this environment, racism isn't seen as a problem; to complain against it is. Therefore, resistance, though cognitively and emotionally costly, is an additional component of work in historically white occupations. To resist and simultaneously engage in emotional labor that maintains comfort in others in the environment comes at a high cost for African American workers in institutionally racialized and gendered organizations—a cost that is beyond the scope of wages. Additionally, because African American inclusion in the industry is represented in token numbers, resistance is thereby collectively shared and reproduced and is an inherent aspect of the microstructures of black flying.

UNDERSTANDING RESISTANCE

Because resistance is a necessary part of life and an everyday part of life in the workplace, crew members must decide if an encounter warrants resistance. This is done through the cognitive process of "picking your battles," as it is commonly referenced by participants in this project. Picking your battles lies in the gravity and frequency of racial encounters. To pick your battles insinuates that you cannot fight every battle, but you should fight those that are most significant at any particular time. One way pilots and flight attendants choose battles to engage in depends largely on the severity, frequency, time, and the perceived intent of the instigator (ignorance or blatant intent). More severe or blatant encounters were often met with resistance. Those encounters that were frequent often called for resistance, or there was the risk of "cosigning on it." Black flight crews noted that if the encounter was repetitive, they felt the need to speak up against it, even if the behavior was not in reference to African Americans but against white women and other groups of color. As poignantly stated by one pilot, but echoed by many,

> It's frequency. If it is something I feel is just really too much. There is this line that I cannot verbalize, but when they cross that line is when I say something. With me, it is how incorrect you are in your stereotypes or racist remarks. If your statement is just too false, I can't take that. It is unacceptable. I don't fight all of the battles because it is not worth it. Some people may not realize what they are saying, and it may be innocent. I don't want to have that angry black man view . . . I don't want to be seen as the problem child with HR. I can't fight all the battles.

Even in this account and the many others contained in this project, resistance is not outside of emotional labor, but it is deeply intertwined in the process. Indeed, the emotional labor performed in the process of resistance is within the boundaries of work and done in a way to reduce the probability of punishment.

Another factor contributing to the likelihood of resistance is the amount of time spent in the company of those making racist remarks. Unlike many other industries, flight crews do not have to interact with the same people on a daily basis as crew members are constantly changing. So, as one senior pilot noted,

> For the most part, I just don't talk about race or racial issues in the cockpit. Ever since I have been pilot in command, I avoid talking about these things because the purpose of conversation is to give information or affect behavior change. And, there is nothing that I can say about race that is going to cause anybody to change within the span of time that they are near me in the cockpit. So I really avoid conversations about race.

Time in interaction was a constant reference crew members used to gauge the necessity of resistance. One other pilot noted something similar: "You can't control ignorance and you can't control someone's bigotry in the amount of time you have with them." For this reason, many were standoffish to engage in heated discussions of race. This notion of changing someone or controlling bigotry is indeed indicative of how these flight crew members interpret the depth of white racism. In these cases, white actors are not receiving a pass based on "they didn't mean it or it is based on ignorance," but there is a tacit knowledge that it takes much more than a few hours to alter beliefs and deep-seated bigotry. We also have to account for the emotional labor that comes through the visceral reaction of experiencing racial prejudices and contemplating the appropriate "battle to pick." The necessary time to decipher which battles to pick in the workplace is but one component of surviving in this type of workplace. If a battle is not fought at the moment crew members experiences racism or sexism, they may indeed carry that emotional burden for hours, even days, before they can discuss this event with sympathetic others.

CONCLUSION

The necessity of understanding the complexities of doing emotion work and emotional labor in the workplace is bigger than engaging in this form of labor with passengers. For black flight crew members, the weight of emotional labor is heavy in the sense that social identity cannot be removed from interactions, specifically those interactions in which others engage in behavior based on identity. The structure of the environment and the demographic makeup of workers and consumers contribute overwhelmingly to the type and frequency of emotional labor that is engaged in by black crew members through resistance. Emotion work is therefore outside of what is systematically required by employers to induce emotion in others, but it often remains "invisible" labor to those not experiencing constant affronts against them based on race and/or gender. We also have to account for the amount of emotional energy expended to experience discrimination and engage in any and all types of resistance. Evident in these accounts of emotional labor and resistance is the *traumatic* nature of experiencing consistent racism and racial oppression and the effect it has on people of color.

Emotional labor is not created equal, but it is indicative of larger structural inequalities found in workplaces. Flight crews have the demands of performing in an atmosphere that largely excludes and alienates them on the basis of appearance as well as devalues the emotions they actually feel. By relying on long-standing gendered stereotypes of black anger, crew members are forced to perform emotional labor within the normative emotional structures reflective of white emotional norms. In this, those avenues granted to white male flight attendants and pilots to express emotions of anger and frustration is not granted to their African American counterparts. This creates a situation in which people of color have to devise an altogether different set of strategies to engage in effective emotional labor and resistance. Additionally, African American men and women are granted different avenues for effective resistance, with men having to navigate the much more stringent reaction of fear to black male anger. Therefore, much of the resistance done by African American males in this environment is done privately, as they are not often granted the option of public resistance.

Perhaps the idea that emotional labor as sold for a wage should cause organizations to question how much emotional labor is worth. For African Americans, emotional labor in white environments is constant and does not begin and end with the start and subsequent end of a flight. These crew members engage in emotional labor from the moment the uniform is on until well after they take it off. It continues through the recounting of stories to other black co-workers and becomes a burden that is collectively shared. Emotion work, however, continues because these crew members are left to cope with heavy and often painful interactions based on their race. Having to constantly be "on guard" while in the workplace presents workers with the obstacle of maintaining a true sense of self in a space where that "self" is not welcomed.

Placing this all in context, even resisting racism does not lessen the "sting" of the event, and black crew members resist and cope with these experiences by performing emotional labor. Recall, too, the cumulative nature of experiencing racism and consider the preparation in the form of emotion work that is required of workers of color in white structural environments. This causes people of color to always be "on" and "ready" for the possibility of being stereotyped, rejected, and/or discriminated against. Indeed, this aspect of silent emotion work remains largely invisible and unacknowledged in the workplace, yet it remains a significant aspect of the type of labor performed by black flight crew members. This labor, when placed in the larger context, becomes much more than managing the hearts of others— it is much deeper and involves much more than managing hearts, for it is much more like managing *lives*.

Chapter Six

Conclusion

For lack of a better term, to succeed, you have to be a chameleon. I don't care what your personal habits are, your personal speech patterns, your behavior differences—when you walk on that property with that uniform you have to be a chameleon—you have to be almost whitewashed. That doesn't mean you change your thinking, but your behavior has to comply with that corporate culture. . . . You have to comply or you will not survive because they can let you go for any reason whatsoever without explanation and you're done. . . . You have to just adapt to your surroundings and imitate. There are forces that do not want to see the status quo overturned. It is the mentality that "you don't belong here, and we're going to do what we can to make sure you don't get here." The airlines' culture was built around that.
—Anthony, senior pilot

The above quote made by a senior pilot captures well the experiences of African American men and women in the airline industry. To be white-washed in order to fit into a corporate culture and survive in the industry is indicative of the daily struggles of going to work and performing a job in which black identity and subsequent labor is not respected. This quote exemplifies the connectivity of cognitive and emotional labor, corporate culture, identity, and the disproportionate ways African Americans engage in emotional labor in this environment. The gravity of feeling involved in the constant negotiation between maintaining a sense of self in an environment in which one constantly feels alienated is expressed through the notion of being a chameleon, or having the ability (or requirement) to adapt and change according to context. As most participating in this project have been employed in the airline industry for at least five years, the process of establishing and performing emotional labor within the corporate structure has been learned through the progression of emotion that often involves taking on more than is given in return. Recall the numerous encounters suffered by black crew members and consider how this process of engaging in emotional labor in the context of work becomes an unfair burden that is required in order to perform the job.

This project has repeatedly shown that African Americans have an altogether different experience in the industry than their white counterparts. Much of their experiences of engaging in emotional labor are a direct consequence of being racially and sexually "different" in a white, gendered environment. Note, too, the marginalization of black voices that take place in organizations with institutionalized practices that value white cultural normativity. By calling out the system of racialized and gendered practices in the airline industry, African American flight crews still maintain hope that there will be an eventual re-creation of the normative structures that now serve to exclude them. The conflict between beliefs of personal rights and liberties and those feeling rules and expectations for emotional labor in the organization is filtered through the complex process of cognitive labor, or the resolution of conflict that can occur between private emotion work and emotional labor. This process, in its entirety, promotes emotional labor as a double shift—it is constantly performed, not only simultaneously with work but also outside of work.

EMOTIONAL LABOR REVISITED: CONTEXT MATTERS

What emerged through my research with black flight crew members suggests that emotional labor has many more dimensions than that proposed by the original theory. To get a more accurate view of emotional labor, this project relied heavily on the rich accounts of African Americans working in two distinct environments within the airline industry. For commercial aviation pilots, specifically those flying for major airlines, there is much education, time, skill, and training involved in entering this field. This contributes to the idea that this position is highly professional. Within this notion of professionalism, there is the overarching ideology that whiteness (and maleness) represents what is professional and indeed remains representative of effective piloting. African American flight attendants are also in a specific location in which to view the ways social identity characteristics interact to create differential access to performing emotional labor. Because this position within the airline industry was and continues to be dominated by white women, African American males and females, like their pilot counterparts, must contend with emotional labor based on those dominant social characteristics. In both contextually gendered occupations, there is an altogether different manifestation of emotional labor when race and gender intersect. Thus, when incorporating understandings of emotional labor, those gendered occupations also become racialized, resulting in the subordination of black male and female emotions.

In the position of flight attendant, racial identity supplants gender, thereby reducing the amount of power and authority granted to black males and females in this occupation.

Because both occupations were formed during a time of widespread exclusion of people of color, an occupational environment representing white cultural norms developed. When African Americans entered this industry, those normative structures were already firmly in place, and through time they have received significant support from those in management as well as consumers. This reproduces those occupational structures that allow for the mistreatment of people of color. Moreover, this research shows that emotional labor does not occur in a vacuum but is contingent on multiple factors. First, the pervasive nature of racism and the white framing of African Americans contribute to their treatment from co-workers and passengers. These interactions, based on racial and gendered stereotyping, are but refurbished versions of those found in years past. Experiences in the workplace cannot be viewed as a specific moment in time, but should be inclusive of how the past meets and influences the present. This research bridges micro-level interactions in the workplace between workers, consumers, and management, with the structural processes that guide feeling rules, emotions, and emotional labor. Indeed, racism and sexism are systemic, with many in mainstream America continually circulating perceptions of the appropriate emotional displays for racial groups. From this perspective we see that emotional labor, unequally placed on workers of color in white structural environments, will perpetually force African American workers to engage in emotional labor with racist and sexist perpetrators. While much of this forced conformity is delegated by passengers, it is even more important to note the amount that comes through interactions with co-workers. In this, emotional labor is constant from the moment the uniform is worn in public to the minute it is removed at the end of the day.

The overall necessity of emotional labor being inclusive of systemic racism is found largely in the continual and documented experiences of African American flight crew members. The previous chapters have documented the consistent interactions between African American crew members, co-workers, and passengers to show that in order to understand *how* people engage in emotional labor, we should also look deeply at *who* they are and what this means in particular environments. This research shows that even though professional status has been achieved, travelers and co-workers do not enter interactions with a blank slate but rely heavily on preconceived ideologies of what black women and men represent. Here, we begin to appreciate the structural mechanisms influencing behavior and the need for emotional labor. Systemic racism and white framing allows the literature to move beyond examinations of the surface interactions that influence emotional labor and peer deeper into much of the emotional labor that can be missed—that labor produced as a result of *forced* social position. Indeed, there is a disconnect between how black workers view themselves and the powerful presumptions of others.

As found in the extensive interviews conducted for this project, emotional labor is much more than what is expected from performing a job and is outside of the scope of what is paid in wages. While the earlier literature only relies on one facet of interactions to understand emotional labor, I suggest that emotional labor occurs in multiple ways in the service industry. Black flight crew members engage in emotional labor that is required of them from management in their professions through interacting with passengers, yet they also engage in emotional labor with co-workers. This aspect of worker-to-worker interaction is largely missed in the literature, yet it is a major aspect of the labor produced on the aircraft. Too, emotional labor for these crew members also involves much more than getting on the aircraft and performing a job. Recall the opening quote in this chapter—it begins the moment the uniform is placed on and one arrives at the airport. Even here, it does not end—flight crew members in this project also note that they continue to engage in emotional labor on layovers and even during their rides to the airport after layovers.

Next, African American flight crew members engage in an altogether different type of emotional labor than their white counterparts. Many of their interactions are based on their positions of being African American men and women. Interacting and engaging in emotional labor and emotion management when attacked based on physical characteristics is a burden that African Americans carry through their invisibility and/or hypervisibility on the aircraft. Much of this emotional labor remains unrecognized and undervalued yet should be highlighted if we are to truly understand the costs of performing emotional labor and render this labor visible. Recall that many of the crew members who spoke against racist and/or sexist behaviors were often sanctioned by co-workers and also by management. They experience emotional labor that is also regulated heavily by passengers and co-workers through their attempts to force conformity.

Through forced conformity, emotional labor becomes much more than a "managed heart." Consider that in much of the literature on emotional labor it is posited that masculinity provides power and authority to men working in "feminine occupations," or the notion that the emotion of anger is usually associated with masculinity in professional occupations. This research argues that emotions are racialized, and in this particular occupation, the freedom to be emotionally expressive through authority and power is removed for African Americans. Their anger is seen as pathological, and problematic, and downright aggressive. Foremost, African Americans do not only manage their hearts, they manage the hearts of those around them. The emotional burden lies in the fact that feeling norms and cultural standards reify whiteness in this occupation. Through the assumed and supported power of whites, *ownership* of black emotional labor takes place. Black emotional labor and emotion management becomes managed.

EMOTIONAL LABOR OF COPING AND RESISTANCE

Collectively, this adds a major component to emotional labor—that emotional labor produced through coping and resistance. There is much information on the coping and resistance strategies of African Americans, but not much is included *within* the emotional labor literature.[1] Being a person of color in an environment that represents whiteness to the workers and travelers produces the necessity to engage in strategies of coping and resistance. Coping and resistance is significant here because it not only adds pressure to black workers, it also takes away much occupational satisfaction. There is considerable time involved in deconstructing racism, accumulating counternarratives, and actively or subtly resisting racism. Much of this emotional labor remains invisible, except to those that perform it on a consistent basis. Experiencing racism and/or sexism is cumulative and uses an extreme amount of emotional and cognitive energy. Even so, African Americans in this project actively resist racist and sexist affronts through a variety of methods, while keeping in mind that they must actively consider the appropriate occasion to engage in resistance. This dimension of emotional labor is not included as an aspect of the job, and it is unrewarded.

Uncovered through this project, African American flight crews must operate and resist carefully or suffer severe consequences. Mentioned in great detail in chapter 5, there are consequences for making claims against racial discrimination that should be considered as an aspect of coping. Here, these flight crew members do not seek to disengage from resistance and reproduce the racial structure, but because many whites deeply adhere to the existing structure, whites reproduce the racial structure, not their black counterparts. In this way, African American flight crew members recognize that racism is not seen as a significant concern by those in management—their complaints are seen as the problem. Much of this is based on mainstream discourse that African Americans are complainers who "play the race card." Within this framework, African Americans collectively fight against the deep-rooted polemic of white management and co-workers.

THE REALITY OF THE (UN)FRIENDLY SKIES

Initially I wanted to be an astronaut. I went to space camp when I was ten years old. When I left space camp I knew I didn't want to be an astronaut, but I knew I wanted to fly an airplane.

> When I was a kid, I was thinking I didn't know anyone that did this. But I
> went to a library and read all of the books on aviation. My parents were very
> supportive, and my mom got me a clipping for Bessie Coleman and that served
> as a mentor. It said, "Negro woman dies in plane crash."
> —Tina, pilot

Tina's story, much like the many men and women in this project, is one of
long-held dreams of being a pilot. Several mentioned knowing they wanted
to fly from childhood, and these stories were coupled with the many years of
training, financial obligations, military service, and setbacks along the way.
Much like Tina, there was an overarching sense of pride between past pioneers and those currently flying as pilot. Darnell made references to the past
when he mentions his start as a flight instructor at a small airport in Texas.
He states,

> I remember before I became a commercial pilot, I did instructing [as] a local
> pilot in my airport in Texas, and when someone needed maintenance done on a
> plane I'd take it to Houston before they [the owner] would get maintenance
> done on it. And some of these planes are worth half a million dollars that
> they'll just give me the keys to go take over it. They'd get out of the plane and
> people would just be like, "Uh, who is flying the plane?" You'd think for a
> second and you think of the Tuskegee Airmen and you just kind of smirk and
> think, it's me!

The connections made between the past and the present and the strong
desire many had to fly should be juxtaposed with the reality of their flight
experiences. From the perspective of emotions, black crew members spoke
of their great enthusiasm of being in the aviation industry, yet they spoke of
their jobs as though the experience in the flight deck is often of loneliness
and isolation. But what often remains hidden behind silenced black voices
and white male supremacy is the many methods through which African
American flight crews are discouraged from advancement. Recall Tina's
example above; she continues her discussion of her experience as a first
officer for her airline. She recalled an encounter in which there were *three*
black female pilots in the same training class, with two of them paired together (they were officially numbers 2, 3, and 4 for the company). During
this time, Tina noted the following experience:

> There are things that they will let slide for others but not for us. I know this for
> a fact, and I know for a fact because of personal experience, because me and
> my training partner, who was also a black female, were in the training depart-
> ment at our initial training for the 737. We had this one instructor, and we went
> in the sim (simulator) and we did our thing for the day, and he commented and
> critiqued us. So I was like, okay, and I asked him if I could go and sit in
> another sim and observe. I was thinking I could maybe pick something up or

something. . . . I went and invited my training partner. So we go in there and it was crazy, and she and I kept looking at each other for the whole two hours of the flight. They were just joking around, and if they missed something, they were like, "Oh, I missed that?" "Yeah, you missed that." The instructors were like, "Oh, that's okay, just make sure you get it next time." The intensity level for them, not that they weren't safe, but the standards that they had were so much less than the standards they had for us. We missed this little button that was not going to cause the flight to end unsuccessfully but it was something that could have been perfected. They were told, "No big deal, you can do it next time." But for us, it was like, "You missed this button; you have to do it again." I know for a fact that there is no way that they are going to let me go up there through [captain] training. If that was my experience as a first officer, I'm not going in there trying to upgrade to captain and not be on top of everything.

When I interviewed Tina for this project, she had been working for this airline for several years, with numerous years of experience before this job working as a commuter captain. Here, she discusses her experiences with training and the likelihood she will go up for captain in the near future. This particular experience, along with many others, has left Tina feeling as though she has to achieve *absolute perfection* before attempting to go up for captain. She also notes that she witnessed other white males in training who did not have to adhere to these strict standards. Noteworthy in this interaction is the idea that this experience has *discouraged* her attempts to move up the ranks. What are the absolute numbers of black pilots who have been institutionally discouraged from attempting promotion or discouraged from entering this industry? In the above examples, emotional labor and the deeper connections between goals, dreams, and the reality of working in an environment in which you are undervalued is yet another manifestation of how emotions are managed in the workplace.

SOLUTIONS AND IMPLICATIONS

Change has been gradual, but one issue that comes back is that the numbers aren't there. They are not there for blacks and Hispanics, but the women are coming up. So part of the issue with diversity will always be exposure and hiring practices, and we need to do better in that regard.
—Tim, senior pilot

In this account, Tim, like many others, notes a distinct reality of the airline industry. Mainstream accounts of employment equality is represented through rhetoric only, but "the numbers aren't there." Tim removes the façade of surface equality by implicitly connecting the lack of diversity in the airline industry with continual hiring practices. As mentioned in chapter 1, many major airlines, as well as other major organizations, now mention the great importance of diversifying their workplace, yet deeper examinations of the industry reveal that diversity, as defined in theory and practice, are not synonymous with equality. Moreover, much of this is mere construct as racial-ethnic minorities and women are likely to remain relegated to lower-level positions.[2] Additionally, though African Americans experience hyper-visiblity in this industry, it is an extreme exaggeration.[3]

One such area for improvement in the airline industry, as well as other structurally white institutions, is through actively seeking, hiring, and promoting qualified people of color. Indeed, it has been only recently (in 2012) that the *second* African American chief pilot was recently named to a major airline, with the first being promoted in 1992.[4] The token numbers of people of color in the industry coincide with the findings here that much institutional discrimination is occurring, and this can only be remedied with institutional practices. In this, there must first be the desire on behalf of those with institutional power to actively seek out gender and racial-ethnic diversity as a major part of the industry. As we continue to expand markets globally, workplace diversity should be representative of the populations they serve.

Second, monitoring any and all claims of discrimination should also be investigated. As mentioned throughout this work, discrimination remains largely unpunished, causing the organizational structure to be reproduced. In another example, a flight attendant mentioned a case in which several flight attendants made a formal complaint against a captain and asked to be removed from the flight when he said to black flight attendants that he "wished somebody would blow up Obama." She continues with "He's still flying." Formal investigations should be conducted, and all those victimized in these cases should be provided with updates on decisions. Indeed, there has been an overarching denial of the rights of racial minorities in the perpetuation of white normativity in the industry as seen through the denial of black claims of racial discrimination. In this, it is important to give voice to marginalized populations in the workplace to elucidate the confounding problems of racism and sexism in this environment. As specific industries become more diverse, it is important that these environments are also inclusive. This would mean going beyond surface policies that include the *rhetoric* of change and acceptance to implementing specific guidelines that reprimand those engaging in discriminatory behaviors. One of the important concerns here is that there is often disagreement between people of color and whites in the amount of discrimination taking place in organizations. Establishing more than an occasional dialogue and/or diversity training initiative, these changes must be continual and be inclusive of all employees, not just those working in specific occupations or positions.

Many of the African American crew members working in this industry often mentioned the desire for more formal networks within the company to mentor young African Americans entering the industry. Indeed, there are outside agencies, such as the Organization of Black Aerospace Professionals and the Black Flight Attendants of America, but many openly cite a need for more avenues to formal mentorship within the industry. Those informal mentoring networks that have developed through a collective understanding of experience should also occur in more formal and organizationally represented ways. Another implication in this research is the need for airlines to get on board in actively engaging in a dialogue with African American crew members. It would suggest recognition of their voices, needs, and suggestions for solutions. African American crew members must be actively involved in creating solutions for a more inclusive work environment. This involvement should be more than surface involvement as our nation's airlines seek an environment promoting equality. There should also be a dismantling of existing organizational structures promoting inequality. It is not until structural changes take place on a large scale that real change can be made. But first and foremost, there must be a grand acknowledgment that racial and gender inequality is a major concern in the industry. This acknowledgment will allow much of the invisible labor performed by African Americans to be noticed and would also provide them with much needed support. As much of the emotional labor in this particular environment results from racialized and gendered interactions with passengers, there should also be a consequence for those passengers openly using racial epithets and/or other derogatory language. As the airline industry has recently been adhering to practices of refusing service based on dress, perhaps this should be extended to passengers that openly use the "n" word or other racial and/or gendered epithets to get the attention of a flight attendant or pilot.[5]

In terms of emotional labor, this form of labor can be extended to other professional occupations that are gendered and/or racialized as a gauge of the overall workplace climate. As there is much time spent in the workplace and in the company of co-workers, these interactions and the resulting emotional labor could easily be extended to examine the experiences of underrepresented and marginalized groups. This research uncovers the various ways in which people of color remain invisible in the industry, and this perspective would fit well through understanding the experiences of Asian Americans, Latinos, and white women in the airline industry, as well as many others. The experiences of these groups with the performance of emotional labor would cement the differentiation of emotional labor in institutionally white spaces. Recall that women, various racial-ethnic groups, and religious groups were a prime source of conversation in the flight deck, and much of the morale of workers is dependent on comfort and inclusion. Many in this project mentioned the connections between experiences with racism and/or sexism and physical illness; it is important to understand the social as well as economical implications of discriminatory workplace practices. Though emotional labor is usually rendered invisible, it is indeed an emotional, cognitive, and physical process, and much more work is needed with respect to the connections between emotion work and the possible physical and psychological consequences.

CONCLUSION

African Americans have made significant progress by entering various industries in which they were historically excluded participation. Entering this particular industry has its costs—both mental and physical. Shown clearly throughout this project, the experiences of African Americans in this industry cannot be fully understood without a closer examination of the organizational structure. Because this industry remains dominated by whites, there are differential expectations for emotional labor that are beyond gender identity to one that intersects clearly with racial identity. The invisibility of the emotional labor performed by workers of color in white industries should be removed if advancements are to be made. Recall those accounts provided in this chapter and note that African Americans have to contend with being "whitewashed" by company standards or are encouraged to seek perfection. These institutional standards, quite unequally placed, remain firmly in place by those with institutional power.

In summation, this current research advances the literature on emotional labor in professional and service occupations. The experiences of African Americans working as pilots and flight attendants for the nation's aviation industry maneuver strict cultural norms that directly contribute to the types of emotional labor they perform. This emotional labor is heavily influenced by racism and sexism that is systemic at the societal and institutional levels. All this labor is performed in addition to the emotional labor required to work in this industry. But one important finding to be gained from this project is on the outskirts of racist and sexist encounters. In spite of these negative experiences, the crew members interviewed in this project take great pride in their jobs and actively seek those personal and collective rewards for remaining in the industry. Of all the painful encounters contained herein, these crew members are resilient, strong, and continue to demand the equal right to keep flying.

Notes

PREFACE

1. I worked as a flight attendant for a major airline from 1999 to 2003, and I officially resigned from the industry in 2007.

2. While a flight attendant, I kept journals documenting my experiences. Though this work is not autoethnographic, I use my experiences as a way to introduce the foundation of the book as rooted in the airline industry.

3. During flight attendant initial training, we received some training and had conversations on the connections between religious ideology and female servers. While we were told that some religious denominations will prefer masculine servers at times, we did not discuss in detail how to handle issues based on race.

4. Sexuality was also missing from the discussion of issues often arising through service.

5. See Arlie Hochschild, *The Managed Heart: The Commercialization of Human Feeling* (Berkeley: University of California Press, 1983).

6. Ibid., 7.

CHAPTER 1

1. Many of the locations mentioned by flight crew members were changed to further protect their identity. Because there are so few African American pilots, it was necessary to provide an additional measure of confidentiality in some cases. When the location has been changed, it will be noted.

2. Identity, as discussed throughout the book, is in reference to the assumptions made by others in interactions and not on behalf of the participant.

Although all of the participants interviewed racially identify as African American, their internal definition of what it means to be African American is not necessarily the focus here. The primary focus is on how "outsiders" define what it means to be African American men and women and how this external definition influences interactions in the workplace.

3. Emotional labor, defined by Hochschild, is that labor done in the context of work to induce or suppress feeling in order to sustain the outward countenance that produces the proper state of mind in others—in this case, the sense of being cared for in a convivial and safe space. This kind of labor calls for a coordination of mind and feeling, and it sometimes draws on a sense of self that we honor as deep and integral to our individuality. This concept will be developed in more detail at various points throughout this chapter. See Arlie Hochschild, *The Managed Heart: Commercialization of Human Feeling* (Berkeley: University of California Press, 1983), 7.

4. See Miliann Kang, *The Managed Hand: Race, Gender, and the Body in Beauty Service Work* (Berkeley: The University of California Press, 2010).

5. I use the term *social reproduction* in this example to signify the fact that the white passenger openly used the racial epithet and was not sanctioned for its use. For the sake of brevity, this concept will be discussed in more detail throughout the book. For more information on the social reproduction of inequality in the workplace, see Kathryn Lively, "Reciprocal Emotion Management: Working Together to Maintain Stratification in Private Law Firms," *Work and Occupations* 27(1) (2000): 32–63; Wendy Leo Moore, *Reproducing Racism: White Space, Elite Law Schools, and Racial Inequality* (Lanham, MD: Rowman & Littlefield, 2008); and Jennifer Pierce, *Gender Trials: Emotional Lives in Contemporary Law Firms* (Berkeley: University of California Press, 1995.

6. Hochschild makes the distinction between those private emotions and the process by which they are incorporated into the workplace with her concept of *transmutation*. Transmutation of "an emotional system" is to point out the link between a private and public act. It is the private act of feeling that can fall under the control of organizations and is profit driven.

7. See Hochschild 1983:18

8. See Hochschild *The Managed Heart*, and Amy Wharton, "The Sociology of Emotional Labor," *Annual Review of Sociology* 35 (2009): 147–65.

9. See Erving Goffman, "Fun in Games," in *Encounters: Two Studies in the Sociology of Interaction* (Indianapolis: Bobbs-Merrill, 1961). This work is cited in Arlie Hochschild, "Emotion Work, Feeling Rules, and Social Structure," *American Journal of Sociology* 85(3) (1979): 551–75.

10. See Kathryn Lively 2000; and Jennifer Pierce 1995 and 2012; and for a succinct discussion on the existing literature on emotional labor, see also Amy Wharton 2009.

11. See Cameron MacDonald and David Merrill, "Intersectionality in the Emotional Proletariat: A New Lens on Employment Discrimination in Service Work," in *Service Work*, edited by Marek Korczynski and Cameron MacDonald, 115 (New York: Routledge, 2009).

12. Ibid., 115.

13. Ibid., 125.

14. Ibid., 127.

15. Ellis Cose, *The Rage of a Privileged Class: Why Are Middle-Class Blacks Angry? Why Should America Care?* (New York: Harper Collins, 1993).

16. Taeku Lee, "Polling Prejudice," The American Prospect.org, March 9, 2011, http://prospect.org/article/polling-prejudice.

17. Many major airlines now post diversity sections to their webpage to show the diversity of their workplace. However, there are no detailed breakdowns of where white women and people of color are located within the workforce. It is suggested that many people of color and women remain in positions that are lower level, even within management. See Janet S. Hansen and Clinton V. Oster, *Taking Flight: Education and Training for Aviation Careers*, Committee on Education and Training for Civilian Aviation Careers, Commission on Behavioral and Social Sciences and Education, National Research Council (Washington, DC: National Academy Press, 1997), and http://www.united.com/web/en-US/content/company/globalcitizenship/ diversity.aspx for information on United Airlines. Currently, there is a major lawsuit, filed by pilots and operations managers at United Airlines, alleging racial discrimination in promotion. See "United Airlines Pilots File Lawsuit Alleging Years of Workplace Race Discrimination," HuffingtonPost.com, http://www.huffingtonpost.com/2012/05/29/united-airlines-pilots-discrimi- nation-_n_1554643.html. American Airlines provides more information on their workforce, yet they also fail to specify the exact locations of diversity within the workforce. More information can be found at http://www.aa.com/ content/images/aboutUs/newsroom/bg_diversity_gen.pdf.

18. Marlon Green was officially the first African American pilot, though he was not the first African American pilot to actually fly commercially. In 1963, Green won his legal case against Continental Airlines and was not reinstated to fly until 1965. Meanwhile, American Airlines hired Dave Harris in 1964, one year after the Supreme Court decision against Continental. See 372 U.S. 714 (83 S.Ct. 1022, 10 L.Ed.2d 84), *Colorado Anti-Discrimination Commission et al., Petitioners, v. Continental Air Lines, Inc.; Marlon D. Green, Petitioner, v. Continental Air Lines, Inc.*

19. See the Organization of Black Aerospace Professionals (OBAP 2012), http://www.obap.org/obap-network/about-obap.

20. See the American Community Survey; see also Rogelio Saenz and Louwanda Evans, *The Changing Demography of U.S. Flight Attendants*,

2009, for earlier 2007 information on the flight attending population, http://www.prb.org/Articles/2009/usflightattendants.aspx?p=1.

21. See Hochschild, *The Managed Heart*, 15.

22. See Eduardo Bonilla-Silva, *Racism without Racists: Color-Blind Racism and the Persistence of Racial Inequality in the United States* (Lanham, MD: Rowman & Littlefield, 2006). Bonilla-Silva discusses color-blind racism as an ideology that explains contemporary racial inequality as the outcome of nonracial dynamics (2). It is a new form of racism that is subtle, institutional, and nonracial (3).

23. See Deborah King, "Multiple Jeopardy, Multiple Consciousness: The Context of a Black Feminist Ideology," *Signs* 14(1) (1988): 42–72.

24. See Joe R. Feagin, *Systemic Racism: A Theory of Oppression* (New York: Routledge, 2006); Joe R. Feagin, *The White Racial Frame: Centuries of Racial Framing and Counter-Framing* (New York: Routledge, 2010).

25. Joe R. Feagin and Melvin P. Sikes, *Living with Racism: The Black Middle-Class Experience* (Boston: Beacon Press, 1994), 75.

26. See Patricia Hill Collins, *Black Feminist Thought: Knowledge, Consciousness, and the Politics of Empowerment*, 2nd ed. (New York: Routledge, 2000).

27. See King, "Multiple Jeopardy, Multiple Consciousness," 72.

28. Labor Force Characteristics by Race and Ethnicity, 2011, published August 2012, http://www.bls.gov/cps/cpsrace2011.pdf; see also Christina Huynh, "Few Women, Minorities in S&P Upper Management Ranks: Report," *Washington Business Journal*, http://www.bizjournals.com/washington/news/2013/03/07/few-women-minorities-in-sp-upper.html?page=all.

29. The purpose of this project is to examine the experiences of African Americans in an industry where they are severely underrepresented in numbers and power.

30. This notion of cognitive labor, or the process of engaging in the private and internal process of pondering, analyzing, and contemplating negative behavior, is manifest through extreme cognitive energy. Because it takes place within the context of work, it is more than emotion work and accompanies emotional labor.

31. In recent research conducted by researchers from Stanford University, the University of Michigan, and NORC from the University of Chicago, the data shows an increase of prejudicial attitudes of African Americans and Hispanics. See "AP Poll: U.S. Majority Have Prejudice against Blacks," USAToday.com, October 27, 2012, http://www.usatoday.com/story/news/politics/2012/10/27/poll-black-prejudice-america/1662067/.

32. For instance, before this time, pilots could step outside of the cockpit and engage in conversations with flight attendants and passengers much more easily than with the new regulations in place.

33. See Feagin, *Systemic Racism*, 7.

34. To introduce the general idea that all emotional labor is based on social identity is not the sole intent here. Because of the nature of the airline industry, there should be an understanding of the overarching emotional labor expectations that most all face in this industry and that are grounded in the nature of the industry itself. There are those cases in which flight crews have to deal with a variety of emergencies, from mechanical and/or medical issues to weather- and passenger-related issues. Thus, I will examine the everyday or ordinary workings and interactions calling for distinct emotional labor on the aircraft and interactions. I include the various emotional dilemmas faced by pilots that go beyond customer service needs, and I include those aspects of maintaining appropriate relationships with co-workers.

35. Respondents for this project were currently employed at the time of our interview and working for major airlines. Major airlines in this case do not include freight carriers or those still flying for the military.

CHAPTER 2

1. Janet S. Hansen and Clinton V. Oster, *Taking Flight: Education and Training for Aviation Careers*, Committee on Education and Training for Civilian Aviation Careers, Commission on Behavioral and Social Sciences and Education, National Research Council (Washington, DC: National Academy Press, 1997).

2. See Margot Hornblower, "The Still Unfriendly Skies," *Time*, August 1995. See also the Organization of Black Aerospace Professionals, http://www.obap.org/.

3. Hansen and Oster, *Taking Flight: Education and Training for Aviation Careers*.

4. See *Colorado Anti-Discrimination Commission v. Continental Air Lines, Inc.*, March 28, 1963. See also *Rogers v. American Airlines*, 1991.

5. Like most other organizations, there is also a hierarchy in place outside of the aircraft. This involves chief pilots (overseeing pilot operations) and management. In this book, discussions of the roles of these individuals will remain in the background as the majority of this project involves the daily operation of the aircraft by the workers on the "front line"—those dealing with the traveling public, before and after the boarding door has closed.

6. See Rosabeth Moss Kanter, *Men and Women of the Corporation* (New York: Basic Books, 1977).

7. See Hansen and Oster, *Taking Flight: Education and Training for Aviation Careers*.

8. See Wendy Moore's *Reproducing Racism: White Space, Elite Law Schools, and Racial Inequality* (Lanham, MD: Rowman & Littlefield, 2008).

9. See Kanter, *Men and Women of the Corporation*, 973, for more information. Though her discussion is on women and their performance within sales occupations, much of this implicitly can be applied to racial-ethnic identity. Even though the occupation of pilot is represented as a masculine occupation, black males are exempt from this classification.

10. See Joe R. Feagin and Melvin Sikes, *Living with Racism: The Black Middle-Class Experience* (Boston: Beacon Press, 1994).

11. See Leslie H. Picca and Joe R. Feagin, *Two-Faced Racism: Whites in the Backstage and Frontstage* (New York: Routledge, 2007), and Erving Goffman, *The Presentation of Self in Everyday Life* (Garden City, NY: Double Day, 1959) for information on frontstage and backstage behavior.

12. For more on the racial uniform, see Robert Park's 1928 work on "Human Migration and the Marginal Man," *American Journal of Sociology* 33(6): 881–93. See also Ronald Takaki's adaptation of racial uniform in *Strangers from a Different Shore* (New York: Little, Brown & Company, 1998).

13. See Joe Feagin, *The White Racial Frame: Centuries of Racial Framing and Counter-Framing* (New York: Routledge, 2010), 137.

14. See Eduardo Bonilla-Silva, *Racism without Racists: Color-Blind Racism and the Persistence of Racial Inequality in the United States* (Lanham, MD: Rowman & Littlefield, 2006), and Feagin, *The White Racial Frame*.

15. The 737 is a type of aircraft flown commercially by many major airlines. In this particular case, the national airline and the airline mentioned by the captain was removed to protect Rob's identity.

16. See Feagin, *White Racial Frame*, for more information on antiblack stereotyping as a white defense.

17. See Jennifer Pierce, "'Racing for Innocence': Whiteness, Corporate Culture, and Backlash Against Affirmative Action," *Qualitative Sociology* 26(1) (2003): 53–70. In this work, Pierce notes that much of the exclusion faced by African Americans in the workplace is through the process of social exclusion.

18. See Bonilla-Silva, *Racism without Racists*, and his discussion on racial narratives. Bonilla-Silva notes that these racial narratives are a part of the story lines found in color-blind racism.

19. See Feagin, *White Racial Frame*, 10–11.

20. Cognitive dissonance, deriving from the tensions between two cognitions, is experienced by many of these African American pilots as they value the right to speak up but are also aware of the consequences. It is the tensions between values of equality and the forced emotional labor manifest through job security/insecurity. See Leon Festinger, *A Theory of Cognitive Dissonance* (Stanford, CA: Stanford University Press, 1957).

21. This ideology (and suggestion) was relayed to me by a senior sociology professor as I discussed some of the excerpts that I received during the

initial testing of my interview guide. This professor asked how those African Americans know what whites "mean" in those interactions. His question was, "Is it possible that African Americans perceive racism because without knowing the thought processes of white actors, it is speculative?" Though many in the academy discuss the racism and discrimination faced by African Americans to be "perceived," it somehow diminishes the "reality" and validity of racism and the voices of those that experience it firsthand.

22. See Joe R. Feagin, *Systemic Racism: A Theory of Oppression* (New York: Routledge, 2006), and Feagin, *White Racial Frame*; and Moore, *Reproducing Racism*.

23. In this account, Anthony provides an angry response that was in many ways aimed at me. Given the opportunity to vent these frustrations, Anthony spoke in a raised voice, pointed, and pounded the table, and in many ways caused me to engage in emotional labor in this interaction.

24. Feagin, *White Racial Frame*, 17.

25. See Bonilla-Silva, *Racism without Racists*.

26. Elizabeth Higginbotham, *Too Much to Ask: Black Women in the Era of Integration* (Chapel Hill, NC: University of North Carolina Press, 2001), 73.

27. Specific locations were changed to protect the identity of the pilot in this story.

28. See Bonilla-Silva, *Racism without Racists*.

29. Ted Nugent, a right-wing musician and activist, has often given interviews laced with racial-ethnic prejudice and sexism. For instance, during a 2007 concert, Nugent said Barack Obama is a "piece of shit that should suck on his machine gun" and followed it up by calling Hillary Clinton a "worthless bitch." Cavan Sieczkowski, "Ted Nugent on Obama Election: 'Pimps, Whores, and Welfare Brats' Voted for 'Economic and Spiritual Suicide,'" HuffingtonPost.com, http://www.huffingtonpost.com/2012/11/08/ted-nugent-on-obama-election-twitter-rant-economic-spiritual-suicide_n_2094490.html.

CHAPTER 3

1. The flight attendant being interviewed did not directly witness this account but relies on a recent conversation she had with an African American female during what they called "venting" sessions.

2. The imagery of African Americans as monkeys is apparent in the writings of Thomas Jefferson in his Notes on the State of Virginia. More recently, many whites have made connections to President Obama, his wife, and children to monkey images. For example, in 2011, Marilyn Davenport, a Southern California GOP official, circulated enhanced photos of the presi-

dent as a monkey with a caption reading, "Now you know why there is no birth certificate." Though many African Americans were upset with the email sent by Davenport, she simply issued an apology for her "unwise behavior," not for the offensive nature of her email. For more information, see Gillian Flaccus, "Marilyn Davenport, California GOP Official, Apologizes for 'Unwise' Obama Chimp Email," HuffingtonPost.com, April 19, 2011, http://www.huffingtonpost.com/2011/04/19/marilyn-davenport-califor_n_850992.html.

3. See Rogelio Saenz and Louwanda Evans, *The Changing Demography of U.S. Flight Attendants*, June 2009, http://www.prb.org/Articles/2009/us-flightattendants.aspx.

4. See Arlie Hochschild, *The Managed Heart: Commercialization of Human Feeling* (Berkeley: University of California Press, 1983), 5.

5. Ibid., 93.

6. See Aimee Lee Ball, "The Colorful History of the Stewardess," CNN.com, January 24, 2011, http://www.cnn.com/2011/TRAVEL/01/24/flight.attendant.history/index.html.

7. See Hochschild, *The Managed Heart*, 97.

8. See Patricia Hill Collins, *Black Feminist Thought: Knowledge, Consciousness, and the Politics of Empowerment*, 2nd ed. (New York: Routledge, 2000), and Joe R. Feagin, *Systemic Racism: A Theory of Oppression* (New York: Routledge, 2006).

9. Yanick St. Jean and Joe R. Feagin, *Double Burden: Black Women and Everyday Racism* (New York: M. E. Sharpe, 1998), 29–30.

10. It is important to note that flight attendants in this project easily differentiated between those who do not accept drinks for other reasons, namely, various religious reasons. But it is important to note the emotional labor involved in these cases as flight attendants "analyze" why exclusionary behavior is occurring.

11. See St. Jean and Feagin, *Double Burden*, 101.

12. Collins, *Black Feminist Thought*.

13. In this example and many others, flight attendants and pilots often mention "deadheading" from one location to another. Usually crew members deadheading have the option of dressing in uniform or in plain clothes. Most times, they will dress in uniform if they are to immediately catch a flight. When deadheading, crew members simply ride as other passengers and are not necessarily at work.

14. In this example, Michelle, like many other flight attendants I interviewed, often used language she perceived I would understand as a past flight attendant. As she mentions "you know how" in terms of the period between deplaning and boarding, she references my collective experience with her in understanding how the "job" works.

CHAPTER 4

1. Here, I would like to thank Joe Feagin for his assistance in developing this perspective. There is a literature that discusses the use of energy in dealing with racism. It is this energy, created as a result of thought and action, that is a part of cognitive labor. Cognitive labor can occur through notions of "picking your battles" as well as in the time associated with developing a narrative and appropriate responses. The resulting emotional labor is not always appropriate, but the cognitive labor used to arrive at the outcome involves deep thought nonetheless.

2. Kathryn J. Lively, "Reciprocal Emotion Management: Working Together to Maintain Stratification in Private Law Firms," *Work and Occupations* 27(1) (2000): 32–63.

3. See Miliann Kang, *The Managed Hand: Race, Gender, and the Body in Beauty Service Work* (Berkeley: University of California Press, 2010); Wendy L. Moore, *Reproducing Racism: White Space, Elite Law Schools, and Racial Inequality* (Lanham, MD: Rowman & Littlefield, 2008); Adia H. Wingfield, "The Modern Mammy and the Angry Black Man: African American Professionals' Experiences with Gendered Racism in the Workplace," *Race, Gender, and Class* 14(2) (2007): 196–212; Jennifer L. Pierce, *Gender Trials: Emotional Lives in Contemporary Law Firms* (Berkeley: University of California Press, 1995); Miliann Kang, "The Managed Hand: The Commercialization of Bodies and Emotion in Korean Immigrant-Owned Nail Salons," *Gender and Society* 17(6) (2003): 820–39; and Adia H. Wingfield, "Are Some Emotions Marked 'White Only'? Racialized Feeling Rules in Professional Workplaces," *Social Problems* 57(2) (2010): 251–68.

4. Wingfield, "Are Some Emotions Marked 'White Only'?" 256.

5. Ibid.

6. See Lively, 2000, "Reciprocal Emotion Management," Wingfield, 2010; Pierce, 1995.

7. See Peggy Thoits, 2004.

8. William A. Smith, Man Hung, and Jeremy D. Franklin, "Racial Battle Fatigue and the MisEducation of Black Men: Racial Microaggressions, Societal Problems, and Environmental Stress," *Journal of Negro Education* 80(1) (2011): 63–82.

9. Jennifer Wang, Janxin Leu, and Yuichi Shoda, "When Seemingly Innocuous 'Stings': Racial Microaggressions and Their Emotional Consequences," *Personality and Social Psychology Bulletin* 37(12) (2011): 1666–78.

10. Smith, Hung, and Franklin, "Racial Battle Fatigue and the MisEducation of Black Men."

11. Derald W. Sue, Christina M. Capodilupo, Gina C. Torino, Jennifer M. Bucceri, Aisha M. B. Holder, Kevin L. Nadal, and Marta Esquilin, "Racial

Microagressions in Everyday Life: Implications for Clinical Practice," *American Psychologist* 62(4) (2007): 271.

12. After having discussions of racist encounters, pilots specifically wanted to point out those positive interactions in order to soften racial incidents. Ironically, when asked of positive experiences, all pilots noted interactions with other African Americans.

13. See Arlie Hochschild, *The Managed Heart: Commercialization of Human Feeling* (Berkeley: University of California Press, 1983), 7.

14. Ibid.; see also Gretchen Peterson, "Cultural Theory and Emotions," in *Handbook of the Sociology of Emotions*, 114–34, edited by Jan E. Stets and Jonathan H. Turner (New York: Springer, 2006).

15. Hochschild, *The Managed Heart*, 190.

16. Ibid.

CHAPTER 5

1. Joe R. Feagin and Karyn D. McKinney, *The Many Costs of Racism* (Lanham, MD: Rowman & Littlefield, 2003); Wendy L. Moore, *Reproducing Racism: White Space, Elite Law Schools, and Racial Equality* (Lanham, MD: Rowman & Littlefield, 2008); William A. Smith, Walter R. Allen, and Lynette L. Danley, "'Assume the Position . . . You Fit the Description': Psychological Experiences and Racial Battle Fatigue among African American Male College Students," *American Behavioral Scientist* 51(4) (2007): 551–78.

2. Patricia Hill Collins, *Black Feminist Thought: Knowledge, Consciousness, and the Politics of Empowerment*, 2nd ed. (New York: Routledge, 2000).

3. James C. Scott discusses the everyday forms of resistance from the perspective of peasantry because many members of subordinate groups do not have the luxury of open resistance and/or political activity. See James C. Scott, *Weapons of the Weak: Everyday Forms of Peasant Resistance* (New Haven, CT: Yale, 1985).

4. Feagin and McKinney, *The Many Costs of Racism*, 51.

5. In the flight deck as well as in the back of the aircraft, there are seats that are unfilled by working crew members. Flight attendants and pilots, not currently on duty, can request to ride the jump seat if it is not already reserved by other crew.

6. See Erving Goffman, *The Presentation of Self in Everyday Life* (Garden City, NJ: Double Day, 1959), for an analysis of frontstage and backstage behavior. See also Leslie H. Picca and Joe R. Feagin, *Two-Faced Racism: Whites in the Backstage and Frontstage* (New York: Routledge, 2007).

7. By stating, "momma gonna give you a good service," this flight attendant engages in emotional labor that in many ways reifies the dominant system. She engages in a gendered dialogue by referencing herself as momma. This was done in a way as to limit the amount of argument that could result from her open resistance by calling herself momma, yet she also places herself in a one-down position in reference to the passenger, thereby reducing her open resistance to something more passive.

8. See Robert T. Carter, "The Relationship between Racism and Racial Identity among White Americans: An Exploratory Investigation," *Journal of Counseling and Development* 69(1) (1990): 46–50. In this investigation, Carter notes that although white women sometimes express racist attitudes, they are more likely to have racial awareness, and this is likely due to their experiences with sex discrimination. The author does not state that white women have no negative attitudes toward African Americans, but in comparison to white males, those attitudes are more complex.

9. See Joe R. Feagin and Melvin P. Sikes, *Living with Racism: The Black Middle-Class Experience* (Boston: Beacon Press, 1994); Moore, *Reproducing Racism*.

CHAPTER 6

1. See Miliann Kang, *The Managed Hand: Race, Gender, and the Body in Beauty Service Work* (Berkeley: University of California Press, 2010), for exceptions; Wendy L. Moore, *Reproducting Racism: White Space, Elite Law Schools, and Racial Inequality* (Lanham, MD: Rowman & Littlefield, 2008); and Adia H. Wingfield, "Are Some Emotions Marked 'White Only'? Racialized Feeling Rules in Professonial Workplaces," *Social Problems* 57(2) (2010): 251–68.

2. See David Embrick, "The Diversity Ideology in the Business World: A New Oppression for a New Age," *Critical Sociology* 37(5) (2011): 541–56.

3. See Charles Gallagher, "White," in *Handbook of the Sociology of Racial and Ethnic Relations*, 9–14. J. Feagin and H. Vera, editors (New York: Kluwer, 2007), for a discussion of the overestimation of African Americans and their social and political progress by whites.

4. See Erica Taylor's discussion of the second African American black chief pilot at http://www.blackamericaweb.com/?q=articles/news/the_black_diaspora_news/36697.

5. Both Southwest Airlines and American Airlines have had passengers removed from flights for "offensive" clothing. In one case, a female passenger was removed for too much cleavage, and in another a pilot reprimanded a passenger for having a curse word on his T-shirt. Also, several airlines do have codes of conduct that can result in a passenger being removed from a

flight. One such policy pertains to any behavior that is abusive, disruptive, or violent. For more information see http://philadelphia.cbslocal.com/2012/08/26/southwest-american-airlines-under-fire-for-dress-code-enforcement/.

References

American Community Survey. 2010. Retrieved December 1, 2011, from www.census.gov/acs/

Ashforth, Blake E., and Ronald Humphrey. 1993. "Emotional Labor in Service Roles: The Influence of Identity." *Academy of Management Review* 18(1): 88–115.

Berg, Bruce L., and Howard Lune. 2009. *Qualitative Research Methods for the Social Sciences*. Boston: Allyn & Bacon.

Bonilla-Silva, Eduardo. 2006. *Racism without Racists: Color-Blind Racism and the Persistence of Racial Inequality in the United States*. Lanham, MD: Rowman & Littlefield.

Brandolo, Elizabeth, Nisha Brady ver Halen, Melissa Pencille, Danielle Beatty, and Richard J. Contrada. 2009. "Coping with Racism: A Selective Review of the Literature and a Theoretical and Methodological Critique." *Journal of Behavioral Medicine* 32(1): 64–88.

Burawoy, Michael. 1991. "Reconstructing Social Theories." Pp. 8–29 in *Ethnography Unbound: Power and Resistance in the Modern Metropolis*, edited by Michael Burawoy, Alice Burton, Ann Arnett Ferguson, Kathryn J. Fox, Joshua Gamson, Nadine Gartrell, Leslie Hurst, Charles Kurzman, Leslie Salzinger, Josepha Schiffman, and Shiori Ui. Berkeley: University of California Press.

———. 1998. "The Extended Case Method." *Sociological Theory* 16(1): 4–33.

Chong, Vincent, Khartharya Um, Monica Hahn, David Pheng, Clifford Yee, and Collette Auerswald. 2009. "Toward an Intersectional Understanding of Violence and Resilience: An Exploratory Study of Young Southeast Asian Men in Alameda and Contra Costa County, California." *Aggression and Violent Behavior* 14(6): 461–69.

Collins, Patricia Hill. 1986. "Learning from the Outsider Within: The Sociological Significance of Black Feminist Thought." *Social Problems* 33(6): S14–32.

———. 2000. *Black Feminist Thought: Knowledge, Consciousness, and the Politics of Empowerment*. 2nd ed. New York: Routledge.

———. 2005. *Black Sexual Politics: African Americans, Gender, and the New Racism*. New York: Routledge.

Cose, Ellis. 1993. *The Rage of a Privileged Class: Why Are Middle-Class Blacks Angry? Why Should America Care?* New York: Harper Collins.

de Jong, Joop T. V. M., and Mark van Ommeren. 2002. "Toward a Culture-Informed Epidemiology: Combining Qualitative and Quantitative Research in Transcultural Contexts." *Transcultural Psychiatry* 39(4): 422–33.

Embrick, David. 2011. "The Diversity Ideology in the Business World: A New Oppression for a New Age." *Critical Sociology* 37(5): 541–56.

Erickson, Rebecca J., and Christian Ritter. 2001. "Emotional Labor, Burnout, and Inauthenticity: Does Gender Matter?" *Social Psychology Quarterly* 64(2): 146–63.

Feagin, Joe R. 2006. *Systemic Racism: A Theory of Oppression.* New York: Routledge.
———. 2010. *The White Racial Frame: Centuries of Racial Framing and Counter-Framing.* New York: Routledge.
Feagin, Joe R., and Karyn D. McKinney. 2003. *The Many Costs of Racism.* Lanham, MD: Rowman & Littlefield.
Feagin, Joe R., and Melvin P. Sikes. 1994. *Living with Racism: The Black Middle-Class Experience.* Boston: Beacon Press.
Festinger, Leon. 1957. *A Theory of Cognitive Dissonance.* Stanford, CA: Stanford University Press.
Gallagher, Charles. 2007. "White." Pp. 9–14 in *Handbook of the Sociology of Racial and Ethnic Relations,* edited by J. Feagin and H. Vera. New York: Kluwer.
Goffman, Erving. 1959. *The Presentation of Self in Everyday Life.* Garden City, NY: Double Day.
———. 1961. "Fun in Games." In *Encounters: Two Studies in the Sociology of Interaction.* Indianapolis: Bobbs-Merrill.
Gough, Brendan. 1998. "Men and the Discursive Reproduction of Sexism: Repertoires of Difference and Equality." *Feminism & Psychology* 8(1): 25–49.
Guy, Mary E., Meredith A. Newman, and Sharon H. Mastracci. 2008. *Emotional Labor: Putting the Service in Public Service.* Armonk, NY: M. E. Sharpe.
Hansen, Janet S., and Clinton V. Oster. 1997. *Taking Flight: Education and Training for Aviation Careers.* Committee on Education and Training for Civilian Aviation Careers. Commission on Behavioral and Social Sciences and Education, National Research Council. Washington, DC: National Academy Press.
Harlow, Roxanna. 2003. "Race Doesn't Matter, But . . . : The Effect of Race on Professors' Experiences and Emotion Management in the Undergraduate College Classroom." *Social Psychology Quarterly* 66(4): 348–63.
Harvey, Adia M. 2005. "Becoming Entrepreneurs: Intersections of Race, Class, and Gender in the Black Beauty Salon." *Gender & Society* 19(6): 789–808.
Higginbotham, Elizabeth. 2001. *Too Much to Ask: Black Women in the Era of Integration.* Chapel Hill, NC: University of North Carolina Press.
Hochschild, Arlie. 1979. "Emotion Work, Feeling Rules, and Social Structure." *American Journal of Sociology* 85(3): 551–75.
———. 1983. *The Managed Heart: Commercialization of Human Feeling.* Berkeley: University of California Press.
Hornblower, Margot. 1995. "The Still Unfriendly Skies." *Time,* August 1995.
Kang, Miliann. 2003. "The Managed Hand: The Commercialization of Bodies and Emotion in Korean Immigrant-Owned Nail Salons." *Gender and Society* 17(6): 820–39.
———. 2010. *The Managed Hand: Race, Gender, and the Body in Beauty Service Work.* Berkeley: University of California Press.
King, Deborah K. 1998. "Multiple Jeopardy, Multiple Consciousness: The Context of a Black Feminist Ideology." *Signs* 14(1): 42–72.
Lively, Kathryn J. 2000. "Reciprocal Emotion Management: Working Together to Maintain Stratification in Private Law Firms." *Work and Occupations* 27(1): 32–63.
MacDonald, Cameron L., and David Merrill. 2009. "Intersectionality in the Emotional Proletariat: A New Lens on Employment Discrimination in Service Work." Pp. 113–34 in *Service Work,* edited by Marek Korczynski and Cameron MacDonald. New York: Routledge.
Martin, Susan E. 1999. "Police Force or Police Service? Gender and Emotional Labor." *Annals of the American Academy of Political and Social Science* 561(1): 111–26.
Mastracci, Sharon H., Meredith A. Newman, and Mary Ellen Guy. 2006. "Appraising Emotion Work: Determining Whether Emotional Labor Is Valued in Government Jobs." *American Review of Public Administration* 36(2): 139–55.
Moore, Wendy L. 2008. *Reproducing Racism: White Space, Elite Law Schools, and Racial Inequality.* Lanham, MD: Rowman & Littlefield.
Noy, Chaim. 2008. "Sampling Knowledge: The Hermeneutics of Snowball Sampling in Qualitative Research." *International Journal of Social Research Methodology* 11(4): 327–44.

Organization of Black Aerospace Professionals (OBAP). 2010. Retrieved September 13, 2010, from http://www.obap.org/obap-network/about-obap/.

Park, Robert. 1928. "Human Migration and the Marginal Man." *American Journal of Sociology* 33(6): 881–93.

Peterson, Gretchen. 2006. "Cultural Theory and Emotions." Pp. 114–34 in *Handbook of the Sociology of Emotions*, edited by Jan E. Stets and Jonathan H. Turner. New York: Springer.

Picca, Leslie H., and Joe R. Feagin. 2007. *Two-Faced Racism: Whites in the Backstage and Frontstage*. New York: Routledge.

Pierce, Jennifer L. 1995. *Gender Trials: Emotional Lives in Contemporary Law Firms*. Berkeley: University of California Press.

———. 1999. "Emotional Labor among Paralegals." *Annals of the American Academy of Political and Social Science* 561(1): 127–42.

———. 2003. "'Racing for Innocence': Whiteness, Corporate Culture, and Backlash Against Affirmative Action." *Qualitative Sociology* 26(1): 53–70.

———. 2012. Racing for Innocence: *Whiteness, Gender, and the Backlash against Affirmative Action*. Palo Alto, CA: Stanford University Press.

Rafaeli, Anat, and Robert I. Sutton. 1989. "The Expression of Emotion in Organizational Life." *Research in Organizational Behavior* 11: 1–42.

Reskin, Barbara, and Patricia A. Roos. 1990. *Job Queues, Gender Queues: Explaining Women's Inroads into Male Occupations*. Philadelphia: Temple University Press.

Romero, Mary. 2002. *Maid in the U.S.A.* New York: Routledge.

Saenz, Rogelio, and Louwanda Evans. 2009. *The Changing Demography of U.S. Flight Attendants*. June 2009. Retrieved from http://www.prb.org/Articles/2009/usflightattendants.aspx.

Smith, William A., Walter R. Allen, and Lynette L. Danley. 2007. "'Assume the Position . . . You Fit the Description': Psychological Experiences and Racial Battle Fatigue among African American Male College Students." *American Behavioral Scientist* 51(4): 551–78.

Smith, William A., Man Hung, and Jeremy D. Franklin. 2011. "Racial Battle Fatigue and the MisEducation of Black Men: Racial Microaggressions, Societal Problems, and Environmental Stress." *Journal of Negro Education* 80(1): 63–82.

St. Jean, Yanick, and Joe R. Feagin. 1998. *Double Burden: Black Women and Everyday Racism*. New York: M. E. Sharpe.

Sue, Derald W., Christina M. Capodilupo, Gina C. Torino, Jennifer M. Bucceri, Aisha M. B. Holder, Kevin L. Nadal, and Marta Esquilin. 2007. "Racial Microaggressions in Everyday Life: Implications for Clinical Practice." *American Psychologist* 62(4): 271–86.

Sutton, Robert I., and Anat Rafaeli. 1988. "Untangling the Relationship between Displayed Emotions and Organizational Sales: The Case of Convenience Stores." *Academy of Management Journal* 31(3): 461–87.

Taylor, Erica. 2012. "Little-Known Black History Fact: Capt. Louis Freeman." January 31. Retrieved from http://tlcnaptown.com/1807892/little-known-black-history-fact-capt-louis-freeman.

Taylor, Steve, and Melissa Tyler. 2000. "Emotional Labour and Sexual Difference in the Airline Industry." *Work, Employment and Society* 14(1): 77–95.

Thoits, Peggy. 1985. "Self-Labeling Processes in Mental Illness: The Role of Emotional Deviance." *American Journal of Sociology* 91(2): 221–49.

———. 2004. "Emotion Norms, Emotion Work, and Social Order." Pp. 359–78 in *Feelings and Emotions: The Amsterdam Symposium*, edited by Antony S. R. Manstead, Nico Frijda, and Agneta Fischer. New York: Cambridge University Press.

Wang, Jennifer, Janxin Leu, and Yuichi Shoda. 2011. "When the Seemingly Innocuous 'Stings': Racial Microaggressions and Their Emotional Consequences." *Personality and Social Psychology Bulletin* 37(12): 1666–78.

Wharton, Amy S. 1993. "The Affective Consequences of Service Work: Managing Emotions on the Job." *Work and Occupations* 20(2): 205–32.

———. 2009. "The Sociology of Emotional Labor." *Annual Review of Sociology* 35: 147–65.

Wharton, Amy S., and Rebecca J. Erickson. 1995. "The Consequences of Caring: Women's Work and Family Life." *Sociological Quarterly* 36: 273–96.

Wingfield, Adia H. 2007. "The Modern Mammy and the Angry Black Man: African American Professionals' Experiences with Gendered Racism in the Workplace." *Race, Gender, and Class* 14(2): 196–212.

———. 2010. "Are Some Emotions Marked 'White Only'? Racialized Feeling Rules in Professional Workplaces." *Social Problems* 57(2): 251–68.

Index

affirmative action, 17, 43; narrative of, 42–44, 47, 107; African Americans; authority, 27–28, 41, 67–73, 77, 89, 96, 109, 123–124; Chief pilot, 128; collective understanding, 22, 91, 94–95, 102–107, 110; discouragement of, 126–127; emotions, 28, 38–40, 44, 82–85, 94; exclusion, 6–8, 12, 15–18, 23, 29, 35–38, 46, 51–52, 58, 70–77, 87, 90, 95, 119, 123; flight crews, 12, 19, 25, 28–35, 40, 44, 47, 55, 68, 78, 79–82, 84–85, 89–93, 99, 101–102, 104–107, 112, 114–116; imagery of, 11, 16, 20, 26, 38, 40–41, 43, 46, 55, 61, 76, 83–85, 97–98, 106; invisibility, 13, 19, 26–27, 29, 48, 124; isolation, 59, 72–73, 75, 76, 77, 90, 126; hypervisibility, 13, 19, 23, 25, 87, 98, 124, 128; networks, 114–117, 128–129; "outsiders", 96; pilots, 6, 15, 16, 23, 24, 83, 94, 97; positive interactions, 94–95; safe spaces, 90, 116. *See also* emotional labor; flight attendants; pilots; resistance

American Airlines, 16
anti-black attitudes, 12
Ashcraft, Karen, 15
Asian Americans, 4
aircraft: confined, 13, 57, 76, 87, 89–90, 99, 107; environment of, xv, 7, 13, 27, 56–57, 76, 95–96, 116, 121; flight deck ("cockpit"), 13, 16, 20, 107; female space, 68, 71; "mini society", 7, 13; white space, 29, 68, 74, 76–77, 84–85, 87, 89, 116. *See also* flight deck

airline industry, xiv, 2; changes in, 56, 58, 75, 97, 103–104, 127; cultural boundaries, 80, 96–99, 101, 105, 113, 117, 119, 121, 128; demographics of, 6–7, 13, 15, 95, 104, 128; flight instructors, 17, 32, 33–35; gender and, 6, 56, 95; history of, 7, 17, 28, 38, 52, 58, 67, 87, 97, 123; management, 39, 63, 86, 89, 96, 99, 123; professionalism, 57, 72, 106, 111, 122; race and, 6, 17, 19, 26, 79; solutions and implications, 127–130; whiteness, 6–7, 13, 15–16, 28, 79, 89, 95, 105, 119, 121, 125. *See also* hostility; white institutional space

Black Flight Attendants of America, 129
Bonilla-Silva, Eduardo, 7

catharsis, 35
Civil Rights Act, 1964, 17
civil rights movement, 58, 80
cognitive dissonance, 38–39, 108
cognitive labor, 12, 79–80, 84, 86, 90, 99, 101–102, 105, 117, 121–122, 125, 129–130
Coleman, Bessie, 126
Collins, Patricia Hill, 61, 66

color-blindness. *See* racism, color-blind
Congress, 43
Continental Airlines, 58
counternarratives. *See* racial narratives
coworkers: exclusion by, 27, 36–38,
    43–44, 60, 68–72; interactions, 7, 25,
    27, 60, 65–69, 72–78. *See also* flight
    attendants; pilots; white institutional
    space
cultural pathology, 32, 84, 97, 105, 124
customer service, xiv, 1, 26, 57, 60, 63;
    during training, xiv, 16

Delta Airlines, 67
denial of service. *See* flight attendants;
    pilots
discrimination: gender, 6–7, 15–16, 17, 41,
    51, 128; racial, 6, 12, 15, 17, 38, 84, 85,
    103, 125
diversity, 7, 32, 77, 128
double shift, 12, 53, 122. *See also*
    emotional labor

Eastern Airlines, 58
emotional burden, 1, 32, 33, 46, 52–53,
    115, 119, 121, 124
emotional energy, 20, 29, 31, 73, 79,
    87–89, 102–104, 107, 110, 112, 119,
    125
emotional "deviants.". *See* emotions,
    deviants
emotional labor: accumulation of, 16, 23,
    28, 74–75, 87, 90–93; cognition, 12,
    38–39, 79, 84, 86, 101–102;
    commodity, 91; constant, 47, 53, 98,
    101–102, 104, 119–120, 122–123, 125;
    context and, 10, 12–13, 41–42, 55–57,
    76, 81, 96, 108, 122–125; costs of, 29,
    35, 72, 85, 89; definition of, xvi, 2–3,
    47, 95; expectations for, 5, 12, 15, 20,
    47, 53, 60, 63, 79–80, 87, 89–90;
    frequency of, 19, 53, 63, 76, 119;
    gendered, 11, 18, 47, 90; invisibility of,
    11, 20, 26, 72–73, 90, 101, 106, 110,
    119–120, 124, 129; multiple
    dimensions of, 11, 12, 15, 18, 19, 41,
    44, 52–53, 57, 59–61, 63, 69–72,
    79–80, 87–90, 95–99, 102, 104–107,
    110, 112–114, 117, 119, 121–125;

personal costs, 11, 20, 30, 41, 85,
    98–99, 101, 114, 117, 119, 130; public,
    2–3, 10–11, 40–41, 55, 64, 70, 73, 75,
    98, 104, 108, 113–114; racialized, 4,
    11, 12, 27, 38–42, 46, 76, 89–90;
    racism, 44, 55–56, 69, 76, 79, 85, 93,
    98, 102, 107, 110, 122; regulation of,
    38, 96, 98, 123–125, 127; resistance,
    12, 78, 95, 99, 101–120, 125–127;
    sexism, 79, 102, 108–109; social
    identity, 7, 11–12, 19, 20, 26, 29, 39,
    42–44, 46, 52–53, 55–56, 58, 66,
    69–70, 76, 80, 89–93, 97–98, 103,
    121–122, 129; structural mechanisms
    of, 79, 81, 97–98, 108, 119, 123;
    unequal distribution of, 7, 32, 42, 53,
    96–99, 104, 106, 119, 123, 129; weight
    of, 80, 89–90, 92, 96, 123, 129; white
    spaces, 81, 89, 92–93, 96–99, 128–129
emotion management, 3, 19, 42, 53, 80, 93,
    95–96, 113; definition of, 3, 95
emotion norms, 3, 11, 12, 53, 81–82, 83,
    86, 89–91, 96
emotional pressure, 40, 59, 97, 101, 125
emotional proletariat, 4
emotional suppression. *See* emotions
emotional supremacy, 5, 6, 83
emotions, 3, 5, 38; anger, 39, 44, 82–87,
    89, 93, 97, 108, 119, 124; conformity,
    86, 89, 96; consequences of, 85;
    definition of, 3; "deviant", 11, 81, 85,
    97–98; frustration, 82, 83, 86, 89,
    91–92, 108, 114, 119; gendered, 81, 87;
    manipulation of, 96, 98; ownership of,
    99, 125; positive, 94–95; racialized, 12,
    29, 30, 38, 81–82, 87, 91, 97, 124;
    stereotypes of, 11, 41, 82–85, 97, 106,
    119, 124; subordination of, 87, 122;
    suppression of, 19, 81, 84, 86. *See also*
    emotional labor; white institutional
    space
emotion Work, xiv, 4, 12, 57, 69, 89–90,
    94, 112–113, 122
exclusion, 12, 17, 21, 38. *See also* airline
    industry; flight attendants; pilots

Feagin, Joe R., 7, 8, 9, 38, 61
feeling rules, 11, 12, 81–82, 96–98, 123;
    definition of, 3; differential, 98;

culturally scripted, 3, 12, 81–82, 96–98

feelings, 3; isolation, 90, 126; norms of, 5, 84, 91, 124

first officer. *See* flight deck

flight attendants: advertising, 57, 64; coworkers, xv, 60, 72–78, 87–69; demographics, 6, 56; denial of service, 1, 6, 63–64, 66, 109; emotional labor, 55–59, 62–63, 66, 70–72, 73, 78, 79–80; emotion Work, xiv, 98; exclusion of, 17, 57, 59, 68–75; expectations of, 56–57, 61–62, 69, 79; gender and, 6, 7, 24, 48, 56–60, 69–71, 96–98, 123; hierarchy of, 67–68, 70, 72–73; hiring, 58; imagery of, 6, 10–11, 24, 56–59, 61, 64–67, 122; invisibility, 57, 64, 67–68, 72–73; males, 62, 69–72, 77, 96–97, 123; passengers, 55, 56, 57, 61, 63, 71; race and, 6, 7, 55–59, 67–69, 96–98; "servants", 60–62, 66, 77; sexualization, 64–67, 77; training, xiv

flight deck,: emotional labor in, 18, 45, 89, 96, 106; hierarchy, 18, 27, 36–37, 46; outsiders within, 89, 96; white-male space, 20, 27–28, 29, 44–46, 48–52, 77, 89, 96, 106–107

flight emergencies, 19

gendered interactions, xiv, 8, 19, 57

gendered occupations, 4, 5, 22, 23, 45–47, 69–70, 87, 95–97, 117, 122, 124

gendered racism, 6, 11, 24, 45, 47–49, 59, 62, 65–67, 70, 97, 108–109

gender uniform, 48, 51

Government Activities and Transportation Subcommittee of the House Committee on Government Operations, 43

Green, Marlon, 6, 16

Haley, Alex, 110

Hansen, Janet, 17, 80

hate stares. See "looks"; subtle racism

Hochschild, Arlie R., xv, xvi, 2, 3, 4, 9–10, 18, 56, 58, 60, 63, 67, 70, 81, 86–87, 95–96, 99

hostility, 35, 41, 42, 44, 93, 101

identity, 2; in interactions, 8, 16; salience, 5, 22, 90. *See also* African Americans; emotional labor; flight attendants

insider, xvi

institutional culture, 2, 12, 89, 97–99. *See also* airline industry; as white; white institutional space

institutional racism, 12, 26, 47, 55; forced conformity, 12; resistance, 12; social reproduction, 12. *See also* racism; white institutional space

institutional support, 88–89, 99, 104

intersectionality, 4, 11, 20, 24, 47, 52, 56, 60–62, 69–70; of emotional labor and systemic racism, 6, 47, 55, 57–62, 70, 79, 89–94, 95–97, 122–123

invisibility, 7, 11, 13, 19, 22, 26, 64, 68, 70–72, 91, 129. *See also* African Americans; flight attendants; pilots

Jim Crow, 62, 103

Kanter, Rosabeth M., 22

Kang, Millian, 4, 18

"looks", 19–25. *See also* racism, subtle

low-wage occupations, 4–5

male bonding, 44–47, 106

The Managed Heart, 9

marginalization, xvii, 6, 19, 38–39, 101, 122, 128–129

Mexican Americans, 44

microaggressions: gender, 16; racial, 16, 92–94

Moore, Wendy L., 5, 17

National Airlines, 58

norms,: gender, 7–8, 28, 50, 53, 61; racial, 6–8, 13, 26, 28, 29–35, 40, 50, 61, 69–70, 77, 83–84, 91, 122

Nugent, Ted, 52

Obama, Barack, 55, 128

occupational segregation. *See also* gendered occupations; racialized occupations oppression, 7, 9, 16, 23, 38–42, 47, 95; interlocking nature of, 16, 41, 47–52, 66, 95–97, 123

Organization of Black Aerospace Professionals (OBAP), 129

organizations: culture of, 11, 19, 79–80, 101; norms of feeling, 3, 5, 11; norms of emotional labor, 5, 11, 63, 79. *See also* airline industry

Oster, Clinton, 17, 80

paranoia, 20, 21, 39, 103, 106–107

Park, Robert, 24

patriarchy. See sexism

pilots: coworkers, 13, 16, 18, 25–29, 29–37, 42–52, 84–86, 88–94, 95–99, 106–110, 111–112, 115–117; demographics of, 6, 15; emotional labor, 16, 19, 21, 52–53, 79–85, 86–99, 121–127; gender and, 16, 19–21, 24, 44–52, 87, 97, 107; imagery of, 2, 6, 11, 15–16, 48–50; passengers and, 1, 18, 19–23, 25, 38–42, 84–85, 94–96, 113–115; racism, 16–17, 24–26, 46–52, 96–98, 106–108, 112–115, 117–120; representations of, 2, 6, 10, 16, 24, 25, 37, 97, 112, 122; training, 16, 29–35; "whiteness", 15, 16, 19, 23, 27, 46, 48, 87, 97. *See also* African Americans; flight deck; emotional labor; racism; sexism; white institutional space

passengers,: deplaning, 39–40, 98, 113; exclusion by, xvi, 21, 38, 41, 56; racism, 25, 41, 57, 58, 63, 113; sexism, 25, 57, 63. *See also* flight attendants; pilots; whites

positive emotions. *See* emotions, positive

prejudice, 35, 37–38, 84, 87, 90, 106–108, 112, 117, 118

race: invisible, xv, 19. *See also* African Americans; flight attendants; pilots

race neutrality, 6–7, 32, 103

racial awareness, 32

racial climate, 89

racial Epithet, 2, 6, 10, 35, 88, 129

racial interactions, 19, 27–42, 59–62

racialized occupations, 4, 23, 30, 40, 46–47, 95, 117

racial markers, 4, 43

racial narratives, 24, 27, 37, 42–44, 56, 66, 103; counternarratives, 79, 101–102, 107, 111, 125

racial uniform, 23–25, 43

racist emotions, 29. *See also* emotions

racist ideologies, 26, 37–38

Reagan National Airport, 1

racism, 7, 24, 25, 44–47, 129; accumulation of, 28, 39, 44, 51, 62–64, 69, 75, 87, 91–94, 120, 125; as motivation, 108, 111–113; backstage, 23, 45; color-blind, 7, 32, 40–41, 79; denial, 26, 128–129; formal complaints against, 103–104, 117, 125, 128; frontstage, 23; longevity of, 94, 102–103, 118; normative nature of, 28, 63, 70, 76–77, 84, 86; overt, 26–28, 39, 46, 55, 59, 62, 77, 82, 93, 101, 113–114; painful reality of, 16, 40, 87, 90, 93–94, 99, 101, 113, 117, 120; physical consequences of, 92, 130; psychological consequences of, 92, 129; reproduction of, 28, 40, 63, 86, 99, 123; stress and, 92, 101; subtle/covert, 20, 21, 23, 31, 34, 51, 73, 93, 101

resistance, 78, 85–86, 95, 98, 117–120, 125–127; active, 103–104, 106–111, 112–113, 117; boundaries (context) of, 104, 108, 113; collective understanding, 22, 28, 95, 102–104, 107, 110, 116, 117; cost-benefit analysis, 102, 107; costs of, 35, 86, 87–89, 98, 104–106, 108, 117, 125; deconstructing white racism, 102–104, 125; defense of "others", 104–108; denial of privilege, 113–114; gendered, 109; micro (passive), 104–105, 108, 109, 111; networks, 114–117; performance, 111–113; picking battles, 118–119; typology of (methods of), 101–102. *See also* emotional labor; institutional racism

Roots. See Haley, Alex

sexism, 7, 12, 16, 39, 44, 44–47, 60, 63, 70, 82, 101, 129

silent suffering, 93

Soul Plane, 41, 114

spatial racism/sexism, 17, 26, 27, 29, 42, 77, 80
spatial segregation, 17. *See also* occupational segregation
stereotypes, 5, 6, 8, 18, 24, 27, 32, 35, 37–38, 56, 60, 97, 102, 116, 123; of emotions, 41, 82–85, 97, 106, 119, 124
Supreme Court, 6, 16
systemic racism, 6–8, 9–10, 15, 17, 19, 26, 28–29, 37–38, 41, 47, 52, 55, 60, 77–78, 79–81, 89–91, 95–99, 103, 123, 130

Taylor, Ruth C., 6
Thoits, Peggy, 81, 84–86, 97
Time, 15
tokenism, 22, 30, 82, 104, 117, 128
training, 29–31; exclusion, 31, 32; gendered interactions, xiv, 52; sabotage, 31, 33–34. *See also* airline industry; flight attendants; pilots
Tuskegee Airmen, 126

United Airlines, 17, 58
unsafe spaces, 27, 32. *See also* white institutional space

U.S. Attorney General, 17

Wharton, Amy, 4
white institutional space, 6, 7, 12, 17, 27, 29, 49, 77, 81–82, 86, 89, 123, 128; forced conformity, 12, 86, 89, 101, 123; reproduction of racial and gender privilege, 12, 27, 28–29, 34, 35, 37–38, 40–41, 50, 63, 77, 82, 86, 89, 97–98, 101, 106, 125; resistance in, 101, 106, 125–127; safe spaces, 27, 32, 40, 45
whiteness,: normative nature of, xv, 6, 7, 25, 27–28, 32, 38–39, 45, 70, 86, 89, 122. *See also* airline industry; flight attendants; pilots
white racial frame, 8–9, 12, 28, 35, 36, 38–39, 58, 60–61, 77, 80, 84, 87, 97, 123; gender and, 8, 49, 58, 60–61
whites: backlash, 41–42, 44, 104; bigotry, 119; cultural norms, 27, 45, 106, 119; emotions, 5, 29, 63, 82, 119; entitlement, 61, 63, 66, 79; males, 44–45, 50; privilege, 27, 41, 45, 67, 70, 75, 79, 86, 106, 113; victimology, 42–43; women, 39–41, 59, 114
Wingfield, Adia H., 5, 82

About the Author

Louwanda Evans is an assistant professor of sociology at Millsaps College in Jackson, Mississippi. In 2012, she received her PhD from Texas A&M University in College Station, Texas. Louwanda's research and teaching interests are primarily in the areas of race, class, and gender and criminology.